Hundred Years of Cooperative Development in India

Hundred Years of Cooperative Development in India

Dr. Lamaan Sami

AKANSHA PUBLISHING HOUSE
NEW DELHI • GUWAHATI • VISAKHAPATNAM

AKANSHA PUBLISHING HOUSE
4649-B/21, Ansari Road
Darya Ganj, New Delhi - 110 002
Ph.: 23263193 / 9811582579 / 09435116718
Fax: 011-23263193
Email: ektabooks@yahoo.com
www.akanshapublishinghouse.com

Hundred Years of Cooperative Development in India

First Published 2011
ISBN 978-81-8370-284-3

PRINTED IN INDIA

Published by Akansha Publishing House, New Delhi and Printed at Harmain Offset Press, Delhi.

Dedicated
to my
Loving Mother who taught me first lesson of
Cooperation.

Contents

Preface

The history of cooperatives in India is more than 100 years old. The canvas of events is far too vast to give it the space it deserves in a book of this size. What I have written is only a brief attempt to recapture the major events that led to the cooperative development as we see today. I have made an attempt to evaluate its progress critically bringing into light the forces that led to its successes and failures in different spheres of its activities and also impact of various commissions and committees on its course of development. No doubt the government as well as members of the cooperatives especially office bearers are responsible for the successes and failures of the movement and its lopsided development.

I am grateful to my teachers viz., Prof. S. U. Farooqui, Dean, Faculty of Commerce, Prof. Badar Alam Iqbal, Chairman, Department of Commerce, Prof. Z. U. Khairoowala, Ex-Dean, Prof. Javed Alam Khan, Prof. Mahfoozur Rehman and my colleagues who have provided help to me.

I am indebted to Prof. R. V. Nadkarni, Prof. R.V. Raju, Mr. M. V. Madane, Mr. R. D. Bedi and other writers whose works have benefited me in many ways.

I feel proud of my father Prof. Samiuddin, a visionary cooperator and writer who has helped me at every stage and provided necessary material for completing the work.

I also place a record the good wishes and necessary help provided by Mr. Mohan Misra, Editor (*Cooperator*), Mrs. Anita Manchanda,

Chief Executive of NCUI, Mr. B. D. Sharma ICA, Ms. Sabitha Venkatesam, Librarian of NCUI, Dr. V. K. Dubey and Mrs. Sonika Nayyer.

Last but not the least, I offer my thanks to those who remained unmentioned but their writings and good wishes have contributed a lot towards the completion of this work.

Dr. Lamaan Sami

1

Pre-Independence Cooperatives (1904-1947)

Origin and Development of Cooperatives

Even before formal cooperative structures came into being through the passing of a law, the practice of the concept of cooperation and cooperative activities were prevalent in several parts of India. Village communities collectively creating permanent assets like village tanks or village forests called Devarai or Vanarai was fairly common. Similarly, instances of pooling of resources by groups, like foodgrains after harvest to lend to needy members of the group before the next harvest, or collecting small contributions in cash at regular intervals to lend to members of the group viz., Chit Funds, in the erstwhile Madras Presidency, "Kuries" in Travancore, "Bhishies" in Kolhapur etc. were to be found. The "Phads" of Kolhapur where farmers impounded water by putting up bunds and agreed to ensure equitable distribution of water, as well as harvesting and transporting of produce of members to the market, and the "Lanas" which were yearly partnerships of peasants to cultivate jointly, and distribute the harvested produce in proportion to the labour and bullock power contributed by their partners, were similar instances of cooperation.[1]

Indian Rural Scenario

Even though the problem of availability of credit was not a new one, it underwent certain changes and assumed new dimensions after the establishment of British Rule and introduction of new land revenue systems which increased the incidence of rent peasants who had tenancy rights over their holding. In the Raiyatwari areas, assessments were revised upwards periodically while in the permanently settled areas abwabs (illegal cases) were realized from tenure-holders. In addition, there was a proliferation of tenure-holders or middlemen who intervened between the government and the tenant. Then, in many cases, tillers of land did not have firm occupancy rights over their holding. The U.P. Zamindari Abolition Committee noted many years later "millions of people were, by these settlements deprived of rights that they had enjoyed for well over two thousand years. Hereditary cultivating properties of land were turned into rack-rented tenants–at will, and conditions were thus created that led to continuous social discord and economic deterioration and the decay of agriculture.

The permanent settlement, contrary to the expectation of many, failed to protect the peasants from arbitraries of Zamindars. In the areas outside Bengal, Bihar and Orissa, initial assessments of land revenue were quite high. They weighed very heavily and in some cases in 1819 it took the peasants nearly 25 years to recover from the crushing effect of the initial assessment. In the Madras Presidency, the state of the peasants was far from prosperous chiefly on account of the very exorbitant land revenue demands.[2]

Because of heavy assessment and the uncertainty of tendency rights, peasants were left with a very small margin of net returns even during normal years. Moreover, they did not have any incentive to invest in agriculture operation. In the years when natural calamities like floods, locusts, droughts and famines occurred, peasants had no alternative but to meet their consumption as well as production needs through loan.

The decline of urban handicraft during British period compelled many of the artisans to migrate to rural areas in order to engage themselves in agriculture as marginal farmers or landless labourers. These people had to borrow even during normal years to meet their consumption needs. In the case of rural artisans, the entry of manufactured goods reduced the demands for their products like clothes, leather goods, utensils and so on. As a result, their economic condition deteriorated and they had to borrow in order to survive.

The moneylenders and traders were the only major sources of credit. Institutional sources were either completely absent or not very significant. Because of their monopolistic positions, moneylenders charged very high rates of interest and put down harsh terms and conditions. Traders saw to it that peasants had no alternative but to sell their produce to them at the rates decided by them, once a peasant fell into debt trap, it was difficult to come out of it. Mounting burdens of interest charges and principal were passed from father to son and so on. These hereditary debts were a big factor in forcing the peasant to remain perpetually in debt. It was said that many Indian peasants were born in debt and lived in debt. At times peasants had to borrow in order to pay off only a portion of interest obligations.[3]

Then there were social obligations like marriage, last rites and various other religious ceremonies and festivals which needed huge expenditure. In view of the prevailing values, attitudes and expectation, it was difficult for a peasant to go in for austerity. Not withstanding various reform movements, extravagance remained the rule rather than expectation. To quote from K. L. Data's Report on the enquiry into the rise of process in India (Calcutta, 1914): In a good year his ignorance and improvidence make him spend the whole of his surplus on marriage and festivities, and his extravagance on such occasions often leads him even in good years to the doors of the money-lenders. A raiyat would stop at no extravagance in marriages and festivities, and his extravagance on such as marrying one of his children or performing any funeral or social ceremony, to show more ostentation than his fellows.

M.L. Darling in his celebrated study on Punjab peasant dealt with this quite at length. He referred to Major Jack's enquiry which had found that it was not uncommon for whole or half a year's income to be spent on domestic ceremonies, and in particular upon marriage. The Famine Commission of 1880 had found the expenditures on marriage and other ceremonies as one of the most prominent course of debt. After a period of four decades it was found that in a typical village of Hoshiarpur (Punjab) almost 40 percent of the original debt had been due to marriage and other social ceremonies. Purchase of gold, ornaments and other such things became a must whenever a marriage was performed and most often money was borrowed for this.

Darling asserted that social ceremonies like marriage, funeral and betrothal were not occasional ones as was believed by some people. In Punjab, a boy is normally married at sixteen or seventeen, and girl a year or two earlier. A family of three therefore means a marriage on the average once every five or six years, and there may be a nephew or niece to marry as well and owning to the early age of marriage there may very well be a betrothal or a funeral. Both will probably cost a sum that in a poor country is not always available.

The debts incurred for social ceremonies were usually very large and unproductive. They were not easy to be rapid. Darling termed a loan for social ceremonies worst because it nails a man tightly down in the coffin of debt.

There were two other causes of unproductive loans contacted by a rural dweller, namely sickness and litigation. The former meant not only expenses or medicines and medical consultation, but also an advance impact on agricultural work if some body of workable age was afflicted with it. Litigation mainly pertained to property disputes and it lingered on for a number of years. Civil cases generally went up to the High Court even if they involved only a fraction of an acre of property, cost huge amounts of money which compelled the rural folk to contract loans.

Darling found that there was a direct relationship between agricultural prosperity and the incidence of debts. This was because land, as a result of the provision of irrigation facilities, had become more productive and was no longer condemned to produce only one crop. Irrigation, especially in canal colonies, had reduced the dependence on the monsoon and, thus, insecurity of harvest. This was true of almost all the areas where irrigation facilities became available or where high value crops came to be grown in response either to national or international market forces.

Obviously, this meant a sharp increase in the value of land. To give an instance, the price of land increased by 24 times on an average between 1866 and 1921-26 in Punjab. In 1862-63, the sale price of land was seven year's land revenue while in 1930 it came 261 years' land revenue. This was not the case in Punjab alone, far away in Champaran in Bihar, where canals were constructed land prices soared up.[4]

Side by side the new judicial system, introduced by the British, increased enormously the hold of moneylenders over debtors. Earlier, they could not get hold of latter's landholdings nor could landholdings be brought to auction, but now everything changed.

The introduction of new land revenue systems and new tendency laws, the decline of the village community with all its traditional importance, strength and power and the establishment of new judicial systems with new laws, rules, procedures and regulations, inaugurated the era of the domination of moneylenders.[5]

Peasants were required to pay up the rents and cesses to either the government or the zamindar concerned on time. They also had to pay interest to moneylenders without default. Thus, they had to rush to the market soon after the harvest to dispose of a large part of their produce irrespective of the price offered. Sometimes they had to sell even standing crops when the need for money became very pressing. A large number of poor peasants and cultivators had to buy back grains after six months or so in order to feed themselves and when they bought back prices were many times higher than what they were six months ago.

The moneylenders who were also dealers in grains lent money, insisting that it should be repaid in grains at the harvest time. Since the prices of grain were lower at the harvest time, they could get more grains. For a long time to come during the nineteenth century, there was no limitation or ceiling on interest rates to be charged by moneylenders. Nor did the government try to regulate money lending business. The question of providing alternative sources of credit never came up to engage the attention of the government till the Deccan Riots took place.[6]

Deccan Riots and Their Perspective

A series of riots took place in 1875 in Poona and Ahmednager districts at Bombay in Deccan. The ire of peasants was directed against the moneylenders-cum-local traders who were generally, Marwaris. The houses of moneylenders were looted and burnt. The farmers demanded the return of their debt bonds and in case this was not done, they were forcibly taken away and destroyed. A great deal of violence took place, which distributed the rural peace in the region. In view of the prevailing circumstances Deccan Riots Commission was appointed which found that there was neither a ceiling on interest rates nor any regulation of money lending business to check malafide practices. Rates of interest were some times 50 per cent or even more. The extent of cultivated land alienated in the two above named districts of Deccan from 4001 acres in 1854 to 10,075 acres in 1874. The Commission found that in Ahmadnagar district about one-eight of occupancy-tenancies were transferred to the moneylenders.

As a result of the recommendations of the Deccan Riots Commission, government brought forth a number of legislative measures. The Deccan Agriculturists' Relief Act (1879) was the first among them. This law had a number of important provisions, designed to protect the debtors. First, it abolished the provision of arrest and imprisonment for debts. Second, it provided for the declaration of the debtor as insolvent and free from all future liabilities once certain conditions were satisfied. Third, it prohibited the alienation of land in order to realize the debt money unless the land was specifically pledged. In addition, the Act, provided for giving back the lands to the debtor in certain circumstances even though a sale-deed was executed. Last, it provided for giving back the lands to the debtor in certain circumstances even though a sale-deed was executed. Last, it provided for a system of village munsifs and boards of concillators of look into the cases involving small amounts of debts and try to bring about amicable and reasonable disposals of such cases. The civil courts dealing with cases of debts were asked to go into the history and the background of loans and arrive at the amount of money which could have been really borrowed. It may be remarked here that it was a common practice on the part of moneylenders to put down a higher amount that the actual sum borrowed. The civil courts were also told to disallow if they thought the amounts and rates of interest were unreasonable.[7]

This Act was amended in 1882 by inserting the provision for the redemption of debts before the due dates, written in debt bonds. Debtors were also authorized to approach the courts for a direction to moneylenders to prove them with detailed accounts of their borrowings and amounts due from them, without seeking the redemption of lands pledged or mortgaged.

As soon as the report of the Deccan Riots Commission became public, it was realized that the same conditions prevailed more or less in almost the entire country. Thus laws were enacted in various parts of the country to tackle the evil consequences of usury and restrictions were placed on the alientation of lands in the event of the failure to repay. The Deccan Agriculturists "Relief Act was extended to the entire Bombay Presidency, after certain modifications.

A Commission was appointed in 1892 to look into the working of the Act. It found, among other things, that the act had worked, to an extent, in favour of moneylenders. The provision for conciliation was misused to the advantage of moneylenders. The government frequently amended the Act in order to rectify its defects, but no sooner the amendments were made then the moneylenders devised ways to evade them. In some cases they tried to overwrite the bonds or acquire the lands under different forms of sub-leases so that the courts did not classify them as mortgages. The working of the Act proved unsatisfactory.[8]

Impact of Debt Legislations

In spite of the fact that the government showed its intention of getting relief to the rural population from the massive burden of debts, the laws enacted in various provinces proved to be inadequate and steps taken under them proved ineffective. This was because the laws were defective and full of loopholes. Moreover there was no uniformity in the laws of various provinces.

In fact, the negative effect of these laws was more glaring than the positive relief to debtors. Since there was no alternative to traditional moneylenders and traders in providing the needed credit, their malpractices could not be checked nor were debtors in a position to put up an effective resistance and ask for the implementation of the provisions of relevant laws. Wherever the government sought to implement the laws and put up restrictions o their malpractices, the result was a contraction in the volume of credit. Most of the moneylenders stopped lending except to their trusted clients.

Most of these measures were corrective, and not preventive ones. Till there was an attack on the moneylenders' monopoly of rural credit, no tangible results could be achieved. Secondly, unlike the institutional credit, no bureaucratic processes were involved for long time consuming formalities which had to be completed when someone borrowed from a moneylender. The latter knows most of this existing and prospective clients and their credit worthiness and depended not only on law but also on his socio-economic position to recover the debts and interest charges. Sometimes, rural population needed credit without delay for medical treatment or funeral or for some other unproductive purpose and in such emergencies, only local moneylender could come to their help.

Lastly, unless the occupation of farming was such as to make a cultivator more or less self-sufficient, his dependence on moneylender could not decline. And for this, a host of measures were needed to be taken from providing irrigation facilities and better inputs to marketing facilities and remunerative prices and the sources of productive loans. Prof. D. R. Gadgil was right in his remarks: 'What was wanted and what alone could really cure the evil, was a positive modification of the terms on which credit was obtained and a salutary check on the purposes for which the cultivator sought credit. No amount of legislation could bring about this result and the only remedy that has been found successful, as yet is the spread of a cooperative credit system and the diffusions among the cultivators of the cooperative spirit.[9]

Government Finance to Agriculture

It is not true that the government did not provide credit to rural population before Independence. It is a different matter that it was very meager and was provided for only limited purposes. Taccavi (or Takavi) loans were a very old form of state assistance to rural population. They were given to peasants to enable them to tide over natural calamities like food, earthquake, fire and famine, etc.

The British government continued the practice of granting taccavi loans and, in some cases, even enlarged their scope. In 1893, it brought forth a number of taccavi loans purposeful. Later on, it promulgated a number of taccavi laws among which the Taccavi Acts of 1871, 1876 and 1879 were significant. No active assistance, however, was given to agriculturists in the matter of credit unntil the Land Improvement Loans Act (1883) and the Agriculturists' Loans Act, 1884 were passed. The latter was framed on the recommendation of the Famine Commission of 1880.[10]

The former was aimed at providing long-term loans to bring about permanent improvements in agriculture. By improvement was meant an activity which increased the letting value of the land and the provincial government was authorized under the Act to decide whether a particular work could be regarded as improvement. The maximum period of repayment was 35 years, but local governments were empowered to fix it within this limit. More often loans were given for 20 years. The rate of interest was fixed keeping in view the rate at which public loans were floated by the government.

The Agriculturists' Loans Act provided for short-term loans to meet current agriculture needs, such as the purchase of seeds, cattle, manure, implements and any other purpose not specific in the Land Improvement Loans Act, but was related with agriculture. Though this Act was not originally supposed to apply only to the times of distress, in practice it became so. The rate of interest was kept so low as to cover the cost of service, and the loans were to be repaid usually at the next principal harvest. A great deal of strictness was observed to make the borrowers keep the time-schedule of repayment.

It was found that the agriculturist have not taken any advantage of these two Acts on any significant scale. This was because of a number of reasons. First, the Acts were to be administered by the collector or the Deputy Commissioner of the district who was always busy with a variety of jobs and responsibilities. He was never in a position to devote adequate attention to the implementation of these acts. Second, in many cases agriculturists were unaware of the existence of these acts and their provisions. Third, a great deal of difference could have been made if loans had been granted on time and this depended on the sincerity of the officials concerned. Most often loans involved formalities and paper work which delayed their actual disbursal. In that case, agriculturist preferred to go to moneylender. Last, a great deal of strictness was shown in the collection of loans.

The Bengal Provincial Banking Enquiry Committee suggested the grant of taccavi loans for the redemption of old debts. In U.P. an amendment was made in 1934 in the Agriculturists' Loans Act, 1884 with a view to include the repayment of existing debts and the purchase of rights in agricultural land among the purposes for which loans under this Act could be provided in U.P. A similar amendment was introduced in Madras.[11]

In short the measures taken by the government neither fulfilled the expectations by way of increasing total production of raw material needed to the British industries located in U.K. nor satisfied the Indians.

Cooperatives: A Possible Solution

Soon after the Deccan Riots, the idea of cooperative credit societies was mooted by William Wedderburn, which found support in nationalist quarters. Justice Mahadev Govind Ranade, for example, was a great votary of cooperative movement. It found champions in Bombay and Poona and even a bill to establish cooperative agricultural banks was moved in the Bombay Legislative Council, but no progress could be made in reality because of the opposition from the Secretary of State. However, its essential features were embodied in the Land Improvement and Agriculturists Loans Acts (XIX of 1883 and XII of 1884) respectively.

The Madras Government was the first in India to be impressed by the reports of the successful application of the cooperative principle in combating the problem of indebtedness in European countries. With a view to exploring the possibilities of its introduction in India, they deputed one of their officers, Sir Frederick Nicholson, "to study the theory and practice of agricultural and other land banks in Europe and to suggest means by which a similar movement may be popularized in India". His report issued in 1895 and 1897 was exhaustive and, was considered to be an invaluable source of information regarding European practices of those days. While Sir Frederick was engaged in this work, another inquiry had been started in the United Provinces to find out the feasibility of establishing agricultural banks in selected areas of the province. An ICS Officer, Mr. Dupernex, was placed on special duty for the purpose and his conclusions were set forth in his book *"People's Banks for Northern India"* published in 1900. He advocated the establishment of village cooperative societies of Raiffeisen type and also of urban banks.

The ideas expounded by Nicholson and Dupernex soon attracted wider attention and some enthusiastic district officers in parts of Punjab, U.P. and Bengal, on their own initiative, started a few pioneer societies. But it was found by experience that unless special legislation was enacted to govern such societies, progress in forming them was not possible; the existing Companies Act of 1882 was too complex to suit them. The serious famines at the close of the century further emphasized the importance of devising adequate steps to meet the requirements of the rural population. Lord Curzon's Government, therefore, appointed a strong committee under the Chairmanship of Sir Edward Law to go into the question and make their proposals.

Before, any legislation was undertaken by the Government for introducing cooperative credit societies in India, Sir Anthony (later on Lord Macdonald) did the pioneering work by establishing in 1901, a number of cooperative credit societies in the United Provinces of Agra and Oudh. Similarly Captain Crosthwaite (afterwards Sir Edward) and Mr. Moclagan had also organized some societies in

Punjab which, at that time, could only be registered under the ordinary company law. At the same time the Government of India impressed with the importance and the future possibilities of the Cooperative Credit organizations appointed a committee in 1901 and consequently the farmer was disinterested in the increasing the yield by putting more inputs as there is a genuine apprehension in his mind that the resultant increased yield would be unjustly appropriated either by the moneylender by making credit more costly or by the landlord by increasing his share in the yield. Before 1901 the government were not unaware of the difficulties which farmers were facing in borrowing funds and had been anxious to ease the situation.

The seriousness and magnitude of the problem attracted the attention of the Government of India in the early eighties. Various measures were adopted to meet the evils of indebtedness. Some aimed at removing the need for borrowing by reducing the land revenue and making its collection less troublesome or by popularizing the Government system of loans to agriculturists. However, the partial failure of the various measures and Acts led those interested in abolishing indebtedness to believe that the sovereign and permanent remedy for the disease lay in the cooperative movement. The principle of operation of the proposed banks was to borrow money at moderate rates of interests from the capitalists whether Europeans on Indians who were willing to lend and to lend it to the agriculturists at a higher rate of interest but never higher than the moneylenders' rate of interest. The loans were popularly known as taccavi loans, but they did not prove a success for they were only granted at the end of much official procedure and delay. Nor were loans granted under these Acts for the redemption of old debts, and when they were granted the system of collection was rather stringent. The security of the loans was the ryots' honesty and industry. The Government of India sympathized with the scheme but when forwarded to the Secretary of State, it was not approved. Sir William Widderburn was the first to review the magnitude of agricultural indebtedness in India and devised practical means to solve it. The thought current started by him has always been the same viz., how to supply the Indian ryots with capital without the loan being the cause of their ruin.

Before cooperative credit societies were given a legal basis and official endorsement, the committee recommended the introduction of a special law to facilitate the promotion of cooperative societies and considered the lines on which such societies should be worked, the privileges which should be accorded to the and the extent to which they should be aided by the Government and subjected to government control. The result, therefore, was that on March 25, 1904 the Cooperative Credit Societies Act was passed to encourage thrift, self-help and cooperation among the agriculturists, artisans, and persons of limited means.[12]

Stages of Cooperative Development

First Stage: 1904 to 1912

The new law passed in 1904 was modelled largely on the English Friendly Societies Act, but was quite simple and elastic. The chief provisions of the Act were: A few persons (not less than ten) living in the same village or town or belonging to the same class or tribe, may register a cooperative credit societies for the encouragement of thrift and self-help among themselves. Societies were divided into two classes namely rural and urban and while the latter were left a free choice, the farmers were bound to accept unlimited liability (except with special sanction by the local government). The main object of the society were to raise funds by deposits from members and loans from Government and distribute the money thus obtained as loans to members. But it might be given only on personal or real security. The organization and control of cooperative credit societies in each province were put under the charge operative credit societies in each province were put under the charge of the special government officer called the Registrar of cooperative credit societies. The accounts of every society were to be audited by the Registrar or by a member of his staff free of charge. The interest of any member in the share capital of the Society was strictly limited and special exemptions from the provisions of the Stamp Act, the Registration Act, and the Income Tax Act were conceded. No dividends were to be paid from the profits of a rural society. The subject of the central banks and the higher stores of the cooperative structure were not, however, dealt with at this stage.

The local government for all the presidencies, and major provinces soon appointed Registrars to spread the cooperative propaganda, to start a few model societies and to train the agriculturists in the proper methods of management and supervision. The Registrars were given full powers to organize, register and supervise societies.

With the passing of this Act, a number of societies came into existence, and within two years (1906-07) the number of societies rose to 843. Their working capital was 23.71 lakhs with a membership of 90.8 thousands. The Cooperative Credit Societies Act, 1904, introduced cooperative legislation in India. Its object, as stated in the preamble, was to encourage thrift, self-help and cooperation amongst agriculturists, artisans and persons of limited means. Societies formed under the Act were authorized to raise funds and carry on business in a cooperate capacity. They were classified as rural and urban; rural societies were required to accept the principle of unlimited liability while urban societies were given a choice of limited or unlimited liability.

In brief, the movement outgrew the expectation of its promoters and the Act was found inadequate to cover non-credit activities. For example, there was no provision in the Act for the formation of Federation or central societies for supervision, control and finance. The basis of classification of the societies into rural and urban was arbitrary. To remedy these and other minor defects, the government of India re-examined the whole provision and passed the Cooperative Societies Act of 1912.

Second Stage: 1912 to 1919

In 1912, another Cooperative Societies Act was enacted to fill the lacuna of the earlier Act. The Cooperative Societies Act II of 1912 was drafted with the intention of removing the deficiencies of the old act while retaining its main features, viz. simplicity, clarity and elasticity. The object of the Act as mentioned in the preamble was to give legal protection and facilities for the formation of cooperative societies for promoting thrift and self-help among agriculturists, artisans and persons of limited means. Thus, provisions were made for the registration of all types of cooperative societies and supervising unions by making provisions for their registration.

The division of societies into rural and urban was removed and substituted by a new division in accordance with the form of liability adopted. The primary agricultural credit societies were to be registered with unlimited liability while central societies with limited liability. It allowed societies to donate money for charitable and educational purposes. The provincial governments were given wide powers regarding the working of societies, settlement of disputes by arbitration and altering byelaws of the societies in connection with the distribution of divided. The use of the word "Cooperation" was prohibited under the Act to any business concern except a society registered under this act. A number of minor improvements were also made in audit and registration, etc.

The immediate effect of the Act was to infuse fresh energy into the movement. New types of societies like cattle insurance, sale of produce, the purchase of manure, retailing farmer's implements and common necessaries sprang up with increased capital and membership. The Government was keenly watching the progress of the movement. To examine whether the movement was developing on sound lines and to suggest measures for further improvement, the government appointed Maclagan Committee in 1914. the number of societies had by 1914 increased to 14,881 the number of members to 6,95,998 and the working capital to Rs. 7,45,31,725. The number of central banks and unions was growing rapidly and the confidence of the public was being won in greater measure. The committee classified societies as (a) primary societies, (b) union, (c) central banks and (d) provincial banks and made recommendations regarding the constitution, financial arrangements, audit and supervision which were adopted by cooperative departments in all the provinces. The committee pointed out the extreme care that should be taken in the formation of rural credit societies and urged the importance of carefully and systematically inculcating the principles of cooperation both before and after the registration of a society. The committee stressed that the area of a primary society should be restricted to village and it should build its own capital by telling members to purchase shares and by persuading them to offer deposits, repayments of loans taken should be strictly enforced according to the instalments fixed, accounts should be regularly audited and provision made for the education of members. With the introduction of Montford Reforms in 1919, after the conclusion of the World War I, cooperation became a provincial subject and the direct responsibility of the Central Government in regard to the determination of policy and conduct of administration of the subject ceased. In 1919, there were 28000 societies with 11 lakh members and Rs. 15 crores was working capital. The progress has been said to be quite rapid.

Third Stage: 1919 to 1929

Under the reform of 1919, cooperation became a transferred subject, under the charge of a minister, in each state. The total number of societies of all kinds in India in 1923 was nearly 56,136. Of these the agricultural cooperative credit societies alone numbered nearly 49,118. Thus, it is clear that the movement has developed almost entirely in the direction of agricultural credit societies. At the same time of the appointment of the Royal Commission on Agriculture in 1926, the number of agricultural credit societies in India was about 65,101. The Royal Commission on Agriculture, with Mr. Calvert as Chairman was set up during this period. The Commission sounded a note of warning in its famous words, "if cooperation fails, there would fail the best hop of rural India." The physical expansion of the movement till 1929, was quite satisfactory. The number of societies increased from 28.4 thousands in 1920 to 94 thousands in 1929. The membership rose from 11.3 lakhs in 1920 to 37 lakhs in 1929 and their working capital went up from 15 lakhs in 1920 to 75 lakhs in 1929.

Rehabilitation was, therefore, quite necessary and several states appointed their own cooperative committee's of Enquiry for that purpose. The Townsend Committee was appointed in Madras as early as 1927 the King Committee of the central provinces and Berar in 1922, the Oakden Committee of U.P. in 1925, the Calvert Committee of Burma in 1928.

Fourth Stage: 1929 to 1939

In 1929, the world economic depression set in and gave the movement a rude shock. The main problems that faced the various committee was to find out a general method of re-examination of loans due to primary societies by individual members, with a view to scaling them down for repayment in easy instalments over a period of 20 years. The large acreage of land that had earlier come into the possession of primary societies and banks in lieu of debts had to be returned on a sort of hire-purchase system. Some of the societies were advised to write off bad debts out of their owned funds, and, if necessary, by resorting to the floatation of debentures.

At this critical moment, some of the provincial governments came forward to give necessary assistance to apex cooperative banks to enable them to supply fresh finance to members of the rehabilitated societies through central banks. They also provided subsidies to meet in particular the cost of management of central banks, in addition to bearing the entire cost of audit as well as the pay of Banking Advisers for a period of five years. There were instances when some of the provincial governments gave cash credits at a low-rate of interest and, in extreme cases, free of interest to tide over the difficulties.

In general the over dues in the societies mounted up and liquidation of societies had to be restored to in certain areas. In Punjab, the Haryana area was the worst affected. Liquidation of societies and recoveries through the process of law were carried out to a great disrepute of the movement. In Bombay, as many as 15000 cases were referred to arbitration. By 1937-38, about 93 percent of loans became overdue. The number of societies in State which stood at 5896 in 1930-31 came down to 4857 in 1935-36. In UP more than half of the societies went into liquidation during the period.

During this period the agriculturists started raising funds on mortgaging their land to local money lenders, a problem which was in existence before 1901. Hence, the first Central Land Mortgage Bank was established in Madras in 1929. Ten primary and one provincial land mortgage bank was established in Bombay in 1935. These banks saved cultivators from the hands of moneylenders, by advancing loans for the redemption of lands and for other long-term needs.

From 1935 to 1939, there were three main developments in the field of cooperation. In 1935, the Reserve Bank of India was established and its Agricultural Credit Department was charged with the duty of studying various problems relating to agricultural credit. In 1936, an All India Conference of Registrars of Cooperative Societies pointedly stressed the need for development of long-term credit through cooperative land mortgage banks. Thirdly, the concept of primary societies being organized as multi-purpose cooperatives came to be increasingly accepted.

Fifth Stage: 1939 to 1947

The period from 1939 to 1947 was wholly connected with World War II. With the emergence of cooperatives having membership from more than one State, such as Central government sponsored salary earners credit societies, a need was felt for an enabling cooperative law that would provide regulatory mechanism for such Multi Unit or Multi State Cooperatives, and make good the inadequacy of provincial cooperative laws too. Therefore, an enabling legislation namely; Multi-Unit Cooperative Societies Act was enacted in 1942, which delegated the power of Central Registrar of Cooperatives to the State Registrars for all practical purposes and regulation of Multi-State Cooperatives. Though there was considerable increase in the price of agricultural commodities, the prices of other consumer commodities rose very high. It was at this time that the cooperative movement began to give much greater importance to production and distribution. Though agricultural societies showed marked improvement owing to the rise in the price of agricultural commodities, marketing societies could not come up to expectation, as there was price control, compulsory procurement of foodgrains and ready market provided at the very doors of agriculturists. A few, however, survived on account of undertaking services like distribution of controlled commodities which was entrusted to them.

The working of land mortgage banks came to a standstill as borrowers made unusually heavy advance repayment which could not be utilized properly. Quite contrary to the happening in the earlier period of the Depression, the central financing agencies showed improvement in deposits and working capital. The overdues also reduced considerably.

This, however, did not last very long. Soon, there was a tendency for fresh borrowing with the result that banks and societies were again short of money. The wages and cost of living also rose considerably. It was at this juncture that government of India appointed, in 1944, a committee known as the policy committee on agriculture, forestry and fisheries to report about the indebtedness of agriculturist and suggests methods to reduce the same. The Committee, with Prof. D. R. Gadgil as Chairman, reported that cooperative developments were not uniform in the different provinces and hence they suggested the establishment of an agricultural credit corporation for each province except those where cooperation was thriving. The cooperative planning committee, with Sri R. G. Saraiya as Chairman, submitted its comprehensive recommendations on all aspects of cooperation in 1946. Following are the important observations recommendations of the Committee on Cooperative Legislation.

"Recommendation No. 212: The experience of working of the Cooperative Societies Act of 1912 and the Acts passed by the provinces has shown that they stand in need of revision in certain respects. It is necessary that the defects in the law should be removed so as to facilitate the smooth working of the plans. The Provinces where Cooperative Societies Act, 1912 is still in force, should pass special Acts keeping in view their past experience and the future needs of the movement. The provinces which have already special Acts should examine their provinces and bring them up-to-date."

The Provincial Governments should also examine other Acts which have a bearing on the cooperative movement and amend them suitably. Where such an Act falls within the legislative jurisdiction of Central Government they should take necessary steps to amend it.

"Recommendation No. 215: a specific provision for appearing against refusal by the Registrar to register a society should be made in the Act as is the case with regard to an order canceling the registration of a society".

Recommendation No. 217: A specific provision should be made for splitting a society into two or more societies and also for amalgamating two or more societies into one without having to liquidate first."

Recommendation No. 222: Any dispute about a person being or not being member of the society should be referred to the Registrar, whose decision should be final. No dispute of this nature should be cognizable by a Civil Court."

Recommendation No. 223: It is necessary to provide for the appointment of a Liquidator to manage the society's affairs till appeal against the cancellation order is rejected or accepted."

The 15th conference of Registrars of cooperative societies, which met in 1947, approved many of the recommendations of Cooperative Planning Committee.

The period 1904-1947, was nurtured by the British Government to ameliorate the conditions of the poor and uneducated farmers. People's initiative was hardly forthcoming. The movement depended mainly on official guidance and support.

There were about 84 thousand primary societies with a membership of 31.75 lakhs, paid up capital of Rs. 14,43 crores, deposits of Rs. 3.11 crores and a working capital of Rs. 21.58 crores. These societies advanced loans in 1946-47 to the tune of about Rs. 9.03 crores and did non credit business involving about Rs. 7.98 crores. There were then 268 primary land mortgage banks with a membership of 1.39 lakhs and working capital of about Rs. 4 crores. They advanced in 1946-47 long-term loans only to the tune of Rs. 66.75 lakhs and the outstanding from them at the end of 1946-47 amounted to Rs. 3.59 crores.

The cooperative movement was in a shaky condition during 1947-1950 although efforts were made to streamline the cooperative development in accordance with the recommendations of Gadgil and Saraiya Committees.

REFERENCES

1. *Report of the High Powered Committee on Cooperatives, 2009*, Ministry of Agriculture, Government of India, p. 5.
2. Girish Mishra, *An Economic History of Modern India*, Pragati Publications, Delhi, p. 116.
3. *Ibid.* p. 116.
4. *Ibid.* p. 119.
5. *Ibid.* p. 119.
6. *Ibid.* p. 120.
7. *Ibid.* p. 122.
8. *Ibid.* p. 122.
9. *Ibid.* p. 131.
10. Romesh Dutt, *The Economic History of India*, Vol. 2, Publication Division, Ministry of Information and Broadcasting, Govt. of India, pp. 131-132.
11. *Ibid.* p. 132.
12. For further details see, Samiuddin & M. Rehman, *Cooperative Sector in India*, S. Chand & Company, Delhi.

2

Post-Independence Cooperatives (1947-2004) *(Pre-liberalization period)*

First Five Year Plan (April, 1951 to March 31, 1956)

The First Five Year Plan (1951-56) outlined in detail the vision of the cooperative movement in India and the rationale for emphasizing cooperatives and Panchayats as preferred organizations for economic and political development. The Plan emphasized the adoption of the cooperative method of organization to cover all aspects of community development. It provided for setting up urban cooperative banks, industrial cooperatives of workers, consumer cooperatives, housing cooperatives, diffusion of knowledge through cooperative training and education and recommended that every government department follow the policy of building up cooperatives.

During this period the recommendation of All India Rural Credit Survey Committee (Gorwala Committee) (1951) which submitted its report in 1954 influenced the course of cooperative development. The Reserve Bank of India Act was amended to enable it to play an active role in cooperative development. The Imperial Bank was converted into State Bank of India. This committee recommended introducing an integrated system of rural credit, partnership of the government in the share capital of the cooperatives and also appointment of government nominees on their boards, thus participating in their management. The Committee emphasized the importance of training. The creation of the State Bank of India was also a major recommendation.

During this plan the All India Cooperative Congress held at Patna in 1956 accepted the principle of state participation and government representation on the Board of Directors of Cooperatives. It resolved that the number of such nominees should not exceed one-third of the total number of Directors or three, whichever is less and applicable even to cooperatives having government share capital in excess of 50% of total share capital. This recommendation was accepted by the Central Government.

Earlier in 1953 the Government of India and the Reserve Bank jointly constituted a Central Committee for Cooperative Training to establish necessary training facilities for cooperative personnel. The All India Cooperative Union and the State Cooperative Unions were entrusted with training of members and office bearers of cooperative organization.

Recognizing the cooperative form of organization as an indispensable instrument of planned economic action in a democracy, the First Five Year Plan clearly expressed preference for the cooperative organization of the economic activities of the people, especially in regard to agriculture, marketing, cottage and processing industries and internal trade, which formed the most important part of the developmental scheme included in the plan. The plan laid down:

"As an instrument of democratic planning, combining initiative, mutual benefit and social purpose, cooperation must be an essential feature of the programme for the implementation of the Five Year Plan. As it is the purpose of the plan to change the economy of the country from an individualistic to a socially regulated on cooperative basis. Its success should be judged, among other things, by the extent to which it is implemented through cooperative organizations".[13]

While the general policy was thus clearly enunciated, the Plan relied mainly on action by the States and the Reserve Bank of India for the development of the cooperative movement.

The plan endorsed the recommendation of the Cooperative Planning Committee to set a target to cover 50 percent of India's villages and 30 percent of rural population in ten years. It was envisaged that by 1955-56, the credit supplied by the cooperative movement and government agencies together for agricultural production should reach the level of Rs. 35 crores per annum Rs. 100 crores as short-term, Rs. 25 crores as medium-term and Rs. 10 crores as long-term loans. The loan operations of cooperative as well as State Governments increased during the plan of the former to an annual level of Rs. 53 crores and of the latter to Rs. 27 crores but actual results were considerably short of the targets indicated in the plan. The main reasons for this shortfall lay in the fact that the cooperative movement was not yet sufficiently broad-based and arrangements for credit were not linked generally with programmes for increasing agricultural production and with schemes of cooperative marketing of agricultural produce. The system of advancing short-term loans with reference to the anticipated crops and production programmes was also not developed to any considerable extent.

While there was significant growth in the number, resources and scale of operations of agricultural credit societies as given below, some of the principal weaknesses of these societies such as small membership, weak capital structure, inadequate loan operations, heavy overdues, failure to harness local savings and to promote thrift etc., continue as much as before progress of the Cooperative Movement during the First Plan Period.

S. No.		1950-51	1955-56
1.	No. of Primary Agricultural Credit Societies	1,15,462.00	1,59,939.00
2.	Membership (in lakhs)	51.54	77.91
3.	Average membership per society	45.00	49.00
4.	Percentage of rural population served	10.30	15.60
5.	Loans issued (Rs. in crores)	22.90	50.16
6.	Average loan per member (Rs.)	45.00	64.00
7.	Average share capital per society (Rs.)	727.00	1,051.00
8.	Average working capital (Rs.)	3,547.00	4,946.00
9.	Average deposits per society	391.00	441.00
10.	Percentage of overdues to outstanding	21.00	25.00

Source: Dr. B. S. Mathur: *Cooperation in India.*

Moreover, the attitude of bureaucracy towards cooperatives, the behaviour of newly born politicians and local leadership was also responsible for this poor state of affairs. There was no agreed policy for the country as a whole nor were any definite targets set, except in regard to the volume of advances to cultivators.

The most important survey in the field of cooperation in India in recent times had been the All India Rural Credit Survey conducted by the Committee of Direction of the Reserve Bank of India. The epoch making report was issued in 1954. It set out the need for coordinated scheme for the development of cooperation in India involving cooperative credit, cooperative economic activity and cooperative education. It recommended that State Governments should draw up plans for the development of cooperative credit in consultation with the Reserve Bank of India and plans for the development of cooperative marketing, processing, etc. in consultation with the Government of India. The state, it said, should enter into partnership with cooperatives at various levels. The recommendations of the Rural Credit Survey were accepted by the Reserve Bank of India, the Central Government, the Indian Cooperative Congress and Conference of State Ministers for Cooperation. Programmes of cooperative development for the Second Five Year Plan of India were drawn up broadly on the lines recommended by this report.

Despite the progress and achievements of the Indian Cooperative Movement, the Report of the Rural Credit Survey frankly criticized the cooperative movement revealing how far it fell short of the urgent economic and social demands of the day. It commented on the failure of the cooperative credit as follows:-

> "For several important reasons, borne out by the experience not only of India but of many other economically undeveloped countries, it may be regarded as axiomatic that at the rural base, that is to say in the village itself, no form of credit organization will be suitable except the cooperative society. Where large production is the aim, the money- lender's credit is obviously unsuitable. The alternative is Institutional Credit, private or other, but this tends more than ever to confine itself to the bigger cultivators if it is not channeled through some form of cooperative association of the borrowers. If, from this statement of a fundamental requirement, we turn to the record of cooperative credit in India, we notice individual instances of success co-existing with substantial failure in quantities term. The foremost objective of policy then becomes the positive and deliberate creation of conditions in which cooperative credit will have a reasonable chance of success".

The reorganization of cooperative credit hitherto made or tried may be described as attempts to rectify the internal weaknesses of the credit structure as a whole, much less its maladjustment to the external mechanism of urban trade and finance. Most reforms of the cooperative movement attempted or affected, have therefore been in the nature of inevitably futile attempts to combine the weak against the strong in conditions in which the weak have had no chance. Thus, effort has been concentrated on thrift, better living, multipurpose societies etc., without the prior preparation needed for correcting the maladjustment between the two economies. The area was cleared for a fight between the weak and the strong with the rules of the game heavily weighed in favour of the strong.[14] The first task is to rectify this position. In other words, conditions must first be created in which cooperation can properly function. No criticism of that functioning is likely to be useful or fundamental unless those conditions are first created. Until then, all endeavour at reorganization will imply the expectation that the socio-economic structure internal to the rural sector will itself create those conditions by cooperative combination, good business methods, etc. That, however, is inherently impossible.

If cooperation did not make much contribution towards the fulfillment of the broad objectives of the first plan, it was due not only to the internal weaknesses of the cooperative structure referred to in the foregoing paragraphs, but also to some extraneous factors. In the fist place, it took quite some time for the cooperatives to appreciate the precise role assigned to them in the development of the economy and gear up their activities accordingly. Secondly, the policy of the States towards cooperation in the new economic setup of the country was not sufficiently defined, except that the general policy was enunciated and action to implement it was largely left to the States and the cooperative movement itself. Finally, the schemes of cooperative development of various states, which were included in their plans, were not uniform in their objects and methods and differed widely from state to state.

There was no agreed policy for the country as a whole nor were any definite targets set, except in regard to the volume of advances to cultivators through institutional agencies. Consequently, there was a marked unevenness in the development of the cooperative structure in different states.

Taimini has rightly said that when officials control and run a cooperative, the facility of participation is denied to the members, which makes the cooperative soulless, an inert government sponsored entity, engaged in some government conceived programme under strict control of Registrar. By the time the second plan was started the stage was set for the budding leaders nursing political ambitions to capture the Cooperative Movement for broadening their base.

Second Five Year Plan (April 1, 1956 to March 31, 1961)

The second plan was committed to the building up of the cooperative sector. The cooperative sector may be distinguished form the private and public sectors. In the private sector there is freedom of action, ample scope for individual initiative and private ownership of property, but side by side it offers scope for exploitation. The public sector, where there is social ownership there is no exploitation by private individuals, but there is neither freedom of action nor there is scope for individual initiative. In either of these, thus, something or other is missing. The cooperative sector, on the other hand, provides scope for both individual as well as social ownership through voluntary action. In this sector, there is full scope for individual initiative while there is hardly any room for exploitation.

The development of the cooperative sector, is therefore, in the best interest of the country. The Third Indian Cooperative Congress, held at New Delhi in the middle of April 1958, also recognized the importance of cooperative sector.

Cooperation was assigned an important role in the Second Five Year Plan as an effective instrument for fulfilling the objectives laid down in the plan. The plan emphasized that:

> "Economic development along democratic lines offers a vast field for the application of cooperation in its infinitely varying

forms. Our socialistic pattern of society implies the creation of large number of decentralized units, both in agriculture and in industry. These small units can obtain the advantages of scale and organization mainly by coming together. The character of economic development in India, with its emphasis on social change, therefore, provides a great deal of scope for the organization of cooperative activity. The building up of a cooperative sector as a part of the scheme of planned development was thus one of the central aims of national policy, which was fully supported by Nehru, the then Prime Minister of India.

The Industrial Policy Resolution of 1956 also affirmed that the principle of cooperation should be applied wherever possible and a steadily increasing proportion of the activities of the private sector had developed along cooperative lines. The resolution emphasized the need for the state to give special assistance to enterprises organized on cooperative lines for industrial and agricultural purposes. It indicated that, in order to realize the objective of a socialistic pattern of society, it was essential "to build up a large and growing cooperative sector".

In pursuance of the policy mentioned above, the plan laid down objectives to be achieved and important activities undertaken by the cooperative movement by 1960-61. The objectives laid down were regarding supply of credit and number of different types of societies to be created. However, no weightage was given to the infrastructure necessary for education, training, legal environment etc. for full participation in the activities of the society.

(i) Supply of agricultural credit through cooperatives

(a) Short term	150
(b) Medium term	50
(c) Long term (outstanding)	25

(ii) Membership of Agricultural Credit Societies (in Millions) 15

(iii) Marketing of agricultural produce cooperatives percent of marketable surplus

To achieve these objectives, the Plan laid down the following targets:

i)	Number of large-sized societies	10,400
ii)	No. of primary marketing societies	1,900
iii)	No. of cooperative sugar factories	35
iv)	Cooperative cotton gins	48
v)	Other cooperative processing units	118
vi)	Godowns of marketing societies	1,500
vii)	Rural godowns	4,000

The scheme of cooperative development is included in the second plan were based on the recommendations of the Rural Credit Survey Committee, the important features of which were:

a) re-orientation of the loan policies of cooperatives so as to benefit the weaker sections of the community, and issue of loans on the basis of production programmes and the anticipated crops instead of the security of landed and other immovable property;

b) strengthening the cooperative credit structure at all levels by state participation in share capital;

c) linking of credit with marketing;

d) development of marketing and processing on cooperative lines;

e) promotion of storage and warehousing; and

f) improving the training facilities and strengthening supervisory and administrative machinery.

As already mentioned the Rural Credit Survey formed the basis of the cooperative plans. Although some recommendations like organization of large size societies and state participation in share capital which brought government dictation had been criticized. Nehru himself once admitted that the L.S. Societies were not advisable for the country. The credit and non-credit societies were to be linked to one another so that whilst the agriculturist is provided with credit and other requirements for actual production, the cooperative movement comes to him for the disposal of his produce. The new policy also revised the terms and loans were to be advanced in terms of the production programmes and anticipated crops, that is, on the ability to repay than on the extent of land owned.

Cooperative farming was to be encouraged as rapidly as possibly so that in ten years or so a substantial proportion of agricultural lands could be so cultivated. The targets were to be set after some initial experience. Considerable flexibility was to be used in the manner of pooling of land and agricultural operation. In these cooperatives, individual farmers may either retain the ownership of these lands or lease it to the society or transfer it to the society. The operation was voluntary and was encouraged by economic inducements.

The promotion of village and small industries through cooperative organization hopes to increase employment, avoid technological unemployment wherever possible and to provide the basis for the structure of an essentially decentralized society. It was also pointed out that the concept of a decentralized society in any country is not necessarily tied to any given level of techniques of production. The entire rural programme is associated with the programmes of land reform with a view to solving the problems of past rural indebtedness and the prevention of future debt.

In the cooperative field, the targets of the second Five Year Plan were no doubt spectacular. The membership of cooperative credit societies was to be raised from 5 million to 15 million. The targets of cooperative credit was to be raised from the prevailing 43 crores of rupees to 255 crores i.e., short-term Rs. 150 crores, medium-term Rs. 50 crores and long-term Rs. 25 crores, 1800 cotton-gins, 118 other processing societies were to be organized. There were to be another 350 warehouses of central and state organizations, 1500 godowns or marketing societies and 4000 godowns of large-sized societies.

Meanwhile, special attention was being paid to strengthen the movement at its base. In 1957, Sir Malcom Darling, an authority on the subject, who had made an earlier report on setting up the Rural Credit Department, came to India under the Colombo Plan and reported on 'recent developments in the field of cooperatives with reference to programmes in the second five year plan' and made recommendations 'for strengthening the organization of cooperative departments in the states, the training programmes for cooperative personnel, and organization of the cooperative movement at and below the district level'.

Sir Malcolm was entirely in sympathy with the recognition of cooperation as the vital principle of rural development but in his report, he uttered a warning not to overstrain the movement in an effort at very rapid expansion.

He argued that the Rural Credit Survey had taken insufficient notice of the regional differences in India, and the 'Second Five Year Plan, following somewhat blindly the Survey Report, takes no account of these differences and seems to expect a more or less universal rate of advance for the whole of India'.

In the five years ending 1951-55 the average membership in the Indian Agricultural Credit Societies had increased from 41 to 46 members. At the time of Sir Malcolm's inquiry only 3 states had an average membership of over 90 and in 6 it was under 34. Already some of the larger societies embraced as many as 20 or 30 villages. Sir Malcolm thought that the target of membership of 500 would not usually be possible for a primary credit society, although larger membership was practical in the case of urban or semi-urban banks.

Sir Malcolm supported his views with the fact that in West Germany's 11,000 village banks the average membership was 155 and in Switzerland's 1000 such banks it was only 110.

Whilst admitting the existing weaknesses of the Indian primary credit societies he proposed an experimental state in increasing the size of societies and in providing direct state aid, and that the results be judged after three or four years.

This process of critical examination of the movement and its path of development was next brought to the forefront of public discussion by resolution of the National Development Council or Cooperative Policy, at New Delhi in November 1958. It raised once again the issue of the appropriate size for a primary society. The resolution came at a time when leading cooperators were having doubts on the wisdom of having official representatives on boards of cooperatives and of increasing the size of primary societies in the hope of thereby creating more viable economic units.

"The council considered that for the development of cooperation as a peoples' movement, it was essential that cooperatives should be organized on the basis of the village cooperative and the village Panchayat. The council recommended that in the light of this general approach, all states should take steps to review their present programmes of cooperative development and formulate fresh programme to be implemented during the next two years. It recognized that conditions differ in different parts to organize the development of cooperative movement along lines set out in this resolution during the course of the next few years.

A working group was subsequently set up with the representatives of the Government, Reserve Bank, Planning Commission and the State Bank to examine the administrative and organizational arrangements for the implementation of the resolution.

The working group, while agreeing with the resolution drew attention to the necessity for some flexibility in the approach to the pattern of organization. Ordinarily a primary cooperative society is to serve one revenue village but in the case of small villages they could be grouped so as to include a population of about 1000. It further held that the credit function which is of primary importance to all the people in the village should not be combined in the same organization with other functions in which only a few people are interested and also with such functions as involve long-term investment or financial risks. There can, therefore, be in addition to the village multipurpose society, one or more cooperative societies in the village for 'specific tasks or specific interests as also cooperative societies covering a group of villages for specific functions'.

The report suggested two patterns of organization to achieve the objectives of the New Delhi resolution:-

Pattern number one which will be one for general adoption, envisages the village cooperative society to be, first and foremost, a service cooperative society with the functions of the provisions of short-term and medium-term credit, supply of agricultural and other production requirements and the marketing of agricultural produce. In addition to these functions, the cooperative society will help to formulate and implement the plan of agricultural production for the village and undertake such education, advisory and welfare activities as may be undertaken by specially well-organized village cooperative by way of extension of their main service functions. But more often, special activities will demand the establishment of separate cooperative organizations. Thus, there may be separate societies for (1) groups of artisans; (2) groups of individuals undertaking activities involving long-term credit, e.g., sinking of a tube-well or running of the cooperatives farm (3) groups of members undertaking activities such as soil conservation, which are of interest to a limited number of individuals (4) activities for which the primary organization has to cover an area larger than a village, e.g., agricultural marketing, and (5) activities involving trading risks, e.g., agricultural marketing, and (6) activities involving trading risks, e.g., the processing of agricultural produce or sale of milk, fruits or vegetables.

The second pattern was for backward areas and areas sparsely populated and also where the growth of the movement has been chronically stagnant. In such circumstance it might be necessary to bring individual societies together into a credit union for the primary purpose of credit itself. Though they are separate legal entities these primary societies and the credit union will be intimately connected in their activities.

The Working Group declared in faovur of forming societies with limited liability but also that there was no necessity to follow a rigid pattern. On state aid the group agreed that there should not be state participation at the village multipurpose society level till the result of the working of 6000 large-sized societies organized so far are carefully assessed. State partnership was to continue in Central and Apex Cooperative Banks as well as other types of societies for marketing, processing etc.

Membership was to be expanded and state aid to villagers in the form of supply of seeds, fertilizer etc. was to be done only through the societies. But expansion in membership should not be pressed on unsound lines or only on paper.

Vigorous thinking and discussion on cooperative problems became a feature of the Indian scene. This was inevitable with the large and rapid changes proposed. The major question of providing rural credit on a much larger scale and in areas hitherto unprovided for came up at a conference of State Ministers for Cooperation held at Mysore in July 1959. In consequence Government appointed another committee, with Shri Vaikunth L. Mehta as Chairman, to examine the subject. It reported in May 1960 that there were as yet no production plans for the village or family in terms of which the expansion of credit could be carried out. It urged that there should be a systematic programme of rectification, consolidation and revitalization of societies.

One of the main aims should be the creation of viable economic units of cooperative service and business. However, the membership should not be too large or its area so extensive as to make the primary society an impersonal institution. An area limit of a distance of three or four miles from the headquarters village was proposed. As for population a majority favoured a ceiling of 3000 i.e., 600 families or 500 cultivating members.

On state aid, Mehta Committee proposed that the State should contribute to the share capital of rural credit societies to the extent of Rs. 1000 to Rs. 10,000 on a matching basis. The society that is partnered by the state should undertake to collect additional share capital of not less than Rs. 5,000 from its members over a period of three to five years. It also recommended a subsidy of Rs. 1,200 from the state for a period not exceeding five years to all viable societies brought under the state programme. The increased share capital as a result of state aid would help the society financially, increasing both its capacity to borrow and to lend.

The Mehta Committee recommended that as a rule mortgage security was not necessary for members loans up to Rs. 500 but such action would be desirable for loans over Rs. 1,000/- the committee considered the existing credit limits of cooperative financing institutions satisfactory but it proposed certain lines for liberalization of credit, including the flow of funds from the Reserve Bank.

The recommendations of the Mehta Committee were generally accepted by the conference of State Ministers for Cooperation held at Srinagar in June, 1960. The Draft outline of India's Third Five Year Plan, issued in June 1960, stated that the programmes under this plan are worked out in terms of the resolution of the National Development Council on Cooperative Policy at New Delhi in November 1958. It reiterated the need for flexibility in organization. Further expansion was envisaged in the programme leading to a cooperative membership of 40 million covering 55 percent of the rural population and as much as 74 percent of the agricultural population.

The Committee on Cooperative Law under the chairmanship of Shri S.T. Raja in 1956 recommended a Model Bill for consideration of State Governments. Another important development, at this time, which affected the cooperative sector, was the National Development Council Resolution (1958). The Resolution on Cooperative Policy stressed that cooperatives should be organized on the basis of the village community as the primary unit and that there should be close coordination between the village cooperative and the Panchayat. The Resolution also recommended that the restrictive features of existing cooperative legislation should be removed. Many State Governments amended their acts, as a result of the recommendations of the Model Bill.

N.D.C. Resolution on Cooperative Policy

The National Development Council in its resolution on cooperative policy (November, 1958) recommended, among other things that:-

(a) Cooperative should be organized on the basis of village community as the primary units and responsibility and initiative for the social and economic development at the village level should be placed fully on the village cooperative and the village panchayat;

(b) The cooperative movement should bring within its fold all villages and all rural families within as short a period as possible and, at any rate, not later than the end of the 3rd plan;

(c) In a rural cooperative, members should have intimate knowledge of one another as well as sense of mutual obligation and concern for the revitalization of the weaker sections of the community. Where villages are too small, with the consent of the communities concerned larger groups could be formed into cooperatives;

(d) Each village cooperative should draw up a plan for increased agricultural production and link the credit programme with the same; and

(e) Taccavi and other loans should be made available through cooperative to create conditions in which every peasant and rural worker would find it to his advantage to join the village cooperative.

Accordingly, the organization of large sized societies was discontinued and the formation of small societies was encouraged.

To determine the question of viability, providing adequate finance and state participation at the primary level an expert committee on cooperative credit was appointed in 1959, under the chairmanship of the Late Shri Vaikunth L. Mehta based on the decisions of the N.D.C and the Mehta Committee Report the Government of India communicated in October 1960 the following important policy decisions:

(a) As a general rule cooperatives should be organized on the basis of the village community as the primary unit. Where villages are too small, the number of villages to be covered by a society may be increased in the interest of viability. The extension, however, is subject to the maximum limits of a population of 3,000 and a distance of a village not more than 3 to 4 miles from the headquarters;

(b) The state may participate in the share capital of primary credit societies, which should ordinarily be limited to Rs. 5,000;

(c) Outright grants at the rate of 3% and 1% of the increase in advances might be provided to primary societies and central banks respectively, from the year 1962-63, to encourage them to lend more and more, to the weaker sections of the community;

(d) Credit should be oriented to production programmes and repaying capacity.

During 2nd Five Year Plan cooperative marketing and processing of agricultural produce formed an important part of the Integrated Scheme of Cooperative Development. About 1900 primary marketing societies were set up and State Marketing Federations were established in all the States, as well as the National Cooperative Marketing Federation at the Centre. Marketing cooperatives along with the agricultural cooperatives played a major role in promoting the Green Revolution by providing credit and inputs to farmers as well as processing their increased outputs.

The Second Plan enunciated that "economic development along democratic lines offers a vast field for the application of cooperation in its varying forms. Our socialistic pattern of society implies the creation of large number of decentralized units, both in agriculture and industry. These small units can obtain the advantages of scale and organization mainly by coming together. The character of economic development in India, with its emphasis on social change, therefore, provides a great deal of scope for the organization of cooperative activity. The building up of a cooperative sector as a part of the scheme of planned development is one of the central aims of national policy".[15]

During the period of first two plans much distortion, corruption and cooptation took the front seat and struggle of the movement utterly failed. The legislation surrounding cooperatives was one of the prime battle grounds when the ICU (now NCUI) confronted the government. Any how the government went on capturing the cooperatives in one way or the other. Nehru was a champion of the movement. He had addressed on different occasions for a clean cooperative movement and right from Lok Sabha debate down to the public meetings, he had explained the need for cooperation and its future shape.[16]

Third Five Year Plan (April 1, 1961 to March 31, 1966)

The Third Plan considers cooperation as a vital factor for social stability and economic growth and visualized wider dimensions for it in the country. The Plan stressed that "Cooperation should become, progressively, the principal basis of organization in branches of economic life, notably agriculture, minor irrigation, small industries and processing, marketing, distribution, rural electrification, housing and construction and provision of essential amenities for local communities. Even the medium and large industries and in transport an increasing range of activities can be undertaken on cooperative lines".

"In a planned economy pledged to the values of socialism and democracy, cooperation should become progressively, the principal basis of organization in many branches of economic life, notably in agriculture and minor irrigation, small industry and processing, marketing distribution, supplies, rural electrification, housing and construction, and the provision of essential amenities for local communities, even in medium and large number of decentralized units in agriculture, industry and the services. Cooperation has the merit of combining freedom and opportunity for the small man with the benefit of large-scale management and organization as goodwill and support from the community. Thus, a rapidly growing cooperative sector, with special emphasis on the needs of the peasant, the worker and the consumer become a vital factor for social stability, for expansion of employment opportunities and for rapid economic development. Along with a growing public and private sector which functions with responsibility to the community as a whole the influence of cooperation extends far beyond the particular activities organized on cooperative lines, and gives to the social structure and the national economy, balance, direction and a sense of value".

Cooperative Credit Targets and Achievement During the Third Five Year Plan

	Short and Medium-term Credit		*Long-term Credit*	
	Target	*Achievement (1965-66)*	*Target*	*Achievement (Loans outstanding as on 30.06.1966)*
Andhra Pradesh	60.00	18.33	23.31	28.32
Assam	8.00	39	1.60	18
Bihar	11.50	10.40	3.50	64
Gujarat	50.00	46.79	20.00	31.71
Jammu & Kashmir	5.00	59	-	16
Kerala	16.00	12.40	3.00	3.09
Madhya Pradesh	40.00	28.89	5.00	4.47
Maharashtra	1,00.00	75.99	50.00	46.06
Mysore	37.50	21.01	10.00	12.84
Orissa	18.00	7.70	2.00	2.72
Punjab	30.00	27.49	2.90	4.40
Rajasthan	18.00	7.73	8.05	91
Tamil Nadu	47.00	30.02	14.48	17.85
Uttar Pradesh	70.00	44.48	5.00	8.13
West Bengal	15.00	8.43	1.50	1.44
Union Territories	3.17	1.41	20	36
Total	5,29.17	3,41.65	1,50.54	1,63.26

Source: T. N. Hajela, *Cooperative in India*, p. 98

In the Third Five Year Plan, an important place was given to cooperation as a major form of organization in many branches of economic activity, especially in the agriculture, small industry, marketing and processing and distribution and supplies. The main schemes of cooperative development in the Plan, therefore relate to the rebuilding and strengthening of cooperative credit structure for the cooperative marketing and processing in conjunction with cooperative credit, provision of godowns for cooperative societies, organization of consumer cooperative stores, development of industrial cooperative societies, strengthening of staff of the cooperative societies and the banks and of the cooperative departments, and making suitable arrangements for training and education in cooperation. Serious efforts were made to develop the movement as an integrated whole both in the second and third plans. As a result, the movement has diversified itself rapidly.

The slight fall in the number of agricultural credit societies from 2,15,081 in 1966 to 2,01,046 at the end of 1964-65 was mainly due to the implementation of the revitalization programme of primary credit societies during third plan period. The membership and working capital however increased considerably. The total short and medium term credit deposit which was Rs. 213 crores in 1961-62 increased to about Rs. 345 crores in 1965-66.

It may be seen from the table that achievements in respect of short-term and medium-term credit worked out to be only 64 percent of targets. In some of the states like Andhra Pradesh, Assam, and Jammu and Kashmir the progress achieved fell considerably short of the targets. The loans outstanding in the central land development banks at Rs. 163 crores as at the end of 1965-66 exceeded the targets of Rs. 150 crores.

Significant progress was registered in the field of marketing and processing of agricultural produce by cooperatives. The value of agricultural produce marketed during 1965-66 was Rs. 360 crores as against Rs. 175 crores in 1961-62. The cooperative societies distributed consumer articles worth Rs. 194 crores during 1965-66 as against Rs. 35 crores in 1961-62. Similarly, the value of agricultural inputs supplied by them also registered an increase from Rs. 40.47 crores in 1961-62 to Rs. 120 crores in 1965-66. From the mid-sixties onwards agro-processing cooperatives, particularly in the sugar and spinning sectors grew in number and contribution, driven primarily by the government's policy of encouraging large scale industries in the cooperative sector and term loan assistance from financial institutions.

There were 52 cooperative sugar factories in production, manufacturing 27 percent of the national production of sugar in 1965-66. A promising start was made in external trade when cooperatives exported agricultural produce of the value of Rs. 96 lakh in 1965-66.

In non-agricultural sector too, cooperatives had shown a significant diversification. Urban consumer stores recorded significant progress during the period. In the wake of devaluation, the programme was accelerated to open new consumer stores and strengthening the existing structures so that the essential consumer goods could be made available at fair prices. During 1965-66, 80 new wholesale stores in the metropolitan and big towns were functioning. The sales turnover of the stores under the centrally sponsored scheme during 1966 amounted to Rs. 160 crores. The daily sales turnover of the department stores exceeded Rs. 5 lakh.

As a result of various steps taken by the Government to sponsor and strengthen cooperatives for weaker sections of the community, various cooperative societies have also come into existence. In 1963-64 there were 5,052 milk cooperatives with 3,48,316 members; 2912 fishermen cooperatives with 2,95,705 members; 1017 labour societies with 9,87,39 members and 9,885 housing cooperatives of various types. In 1964-65, there were 4,000 labour contract and construction cooperatives with a local membership of 2,078 lakhs. In the same year, the number of industrial cooperatives was about 51,000 with a value of sales of Rs. 117 crores. About 50 per cent of the handlooms in the country are in the cooperative sector.

The Chinese aggression gave a rude shock to the economy. Priorities were changed. After the Indo-China war in 1962, both the Consumer Cooperative Structure and the Public Distribution System (PDS) was strengthened. The government as a matter of policy decided to give preference to consumer or other cooperatives in the allotment of fair price shops and certain states allotted new fair price shops only to cooperatives.

With the growth of public deposits in Urban Cooperative Credit Societies, it was felt necessary to insure these under the Deposit Insurance Scheme of Reserve Bank of India. Selective provisions of the RBI Act 1934 and later Banking Regulation Act 1949 were made applicable to Cooperative Banks w.e.f. March 1, 1966 to regulate their banking business and facilitate insurance coverage of deposits. Thus, they became an integral part of the banking system of the country.

With the setting up of NDDB to replicate the Anand pattern of cooperatives in milk, the Indian dairy cooperative movement received a spurt. Later on NDDB also ventured into the field of edible oils.

Later on Pakistan's invasion brought a chock wave. However, the cooperatives were not adversely affected as a whole. In certain cooperative sectors like consumers and industrial a marked improvement was made. Although the movement proposed the economy was jeopardized during the plan. The third plan saw birth after NMNICM (1967) NCDC (1963). Along with growth of consumers cooperatives, the growth of land development banks, rural electrical cooperatives and programmes for clarity, poultry, fishery and labour cooperatives were set up.

Fourth Five Year Plan (April 1, 1969 to March 31, 1974)

The Third Five Year Economic Plan of India ended in 1965-66

and the Fourth should have been started in 1966-67. In view of a number of developments during the Third Plan, namely the hostilities of 1962 and 1965, widespread drought in 1965-66 and 1966-67 and a strained foreign exchange situation, the Indian Planning Commission decided that the fourth Plan should commence in 1969-70. Meanwhile development was kept going on in terms of annual plans from 1966-67 to 1968-69.

During the period 1966-68, an important development in India was the implementation of the new agricultural strategy which aimed at self-sufficiency in food by 1970-71. The main plank of the new strategy was the highly yielding varieties programme which (according to the Reserve Bank's Report on the Cooperative) was initiated from the Kharif season of 1956. This programme had good results but was inhibited because of an inadequate response from the cooperatives. Despite the re-organization of the cooperative credit institutions since the Second Five Year Plan through state participation and assistance from the Reserve Bank of India and the Central Government the credit structure in most of the states of India continued to be weak.

The Reserve Bank of India observed that "Cooperative credit institutions, especially central cooperative banks and primary agricultural credit societies in several states, continued to be in a state of stagnation. The position of overdues and operational efficiency in a few central banks deteriorated to such an extent that they could no longer serve as effective channels for the flow of credit from higher financing agencies. The Reserve Bank therefore advised some of the State Governments to draw up special programme for the rehabilitation of a few central banks and their affiliated societies, which involved an evaluation of bad and doubtful debts with the help of special staff, recovery of overdue loans, toning of their administration and working etc. In fact, sanction of credit limits to these banks by the Reserve Bank was made conditional to the state governments concerned taking necessary steps for rehabilitating the credit institutions on certain lines".

The Congress emphasized the use of the Cooperative form of organization in the planned economic development and called for an expanded role in the Fourth Five Year Plan. It drew attention to the need for intensive training of cooperative personnel. During the period 1966-67, there were also two conferences of the State Chief Ministers and Ministers of Cooperation.

The All India Rural Credit Review Committee, which was constituted by the Reserve Bank of India in 1966, was also active. In its report made in February and July 1969 recommended, among other things, the establishment of a statutory Agricultural Credit Board in the Reserve Bank of India, the setting up of a Small Farmer's Development Agency in selected districts, a Rural Electrification Corporation, the expansion of the role of the Agricultural Refinance Corporation and measures for the flow of adequate and timely credit for agriculture.

The Standing Advisory Committee on Rural and Cooperative Credit constituted by the Reserve Bank for advising the Bank on agricultural credit met four times during 1966-68 and examined the problems of Industrial cooperative banks, medium-term loans for agriculture and the question of the appointment of Registrars of Cooperative Societies. It noted with concern the frequent change of Registrars in some states and the inadequacy of their specialized training.

Rules known as the Banking Regulation (Cooperative Societies) Rules 1966 were framed under India's Banking Regulations Act, 1949. Under these rules every cooperative bank, in addition to average daily balances required to be maintained by a scheduled state cooperative bank, or cash reserves required to be maintained by every other cooperative bank, will have to maintain liquid assets which should not be less than 25 percent of the total of its demand and time liabilities in India.

Growth with stability was expected to be the keynote of the cooperative movement during the Fourth Plan. Agricultural Cooperative and consumer societies are accorded a central position in the strategy of cooperative development. The Fourth Plan aimed to ensure that the services which farmers required were institutionalized to the greatest extent possible. The target of this Plan was to bring the entire village and ¾ of population under cooperation. The Plan ensured that cooperatives are being helped to equip themselves in important aspects like finance, organization and trained personnel.[17]

So far as cooperative development is concerned, the Fourth Plan envisages an outlay of Rs. 178.57 crores distributed as under:

Outlay on Cooperative Development Programme during Fourth Plan

S.No.		*Outlay (Rs. Crore)*
1.	States	119.21
2.	Union Territories	4.61
3.	Centrally sponsored	24.50
4.	Central Sector	30.25
	Total	178.57

Source: Hejela T.N. *Op.cit*, p. 99

In addition, the outlay under the Central sector includes a provision of Rs. 90 crores separately made for support to debentures of land development banks. The document also set out in detail the approach to policy and programme of cooperative development during the Fourth Plan period".[18]

This plan was much influenced by the recommendations of All India Rural Credit Review Committee (1969) which recommended reorganization of rural credit in the Reserve Bank, setting up of a small farmers development agency, creation of rural electrification corporation, adoption of various measures for timely and adequate flow of credit.[19]

The fourth plan had emphasized on reorganization of primary credit structure, rehabilitation of weak central banks, reduction of over and mobilization of deposits. The loaning policy of credit societies and land development banks also underwent changes in favour of small farmers.

Cooperative marketing, processing and consumers stores were also emphasized during the plan. Stress was laid on consolidation and strengthening of primary and central consumer cooperatives and state as well as national federations. The cooperatives were involved in rural electrification programme. Other forms of cooperatives were also encouraged.

On the recommendation of a working group on Industrial Cooperatives (1963) for the Fourth Plan, the village and small industries in the cooperative sector were encouraged whenever appropriate.

As majority of cooperative industries were managed by personnel on deputation from government, who had no stake in the growth of cooperative institution and lacked business aptitude, the fourth plan emphasized the importance of cadre and decided for the creation of nucleus pools of senior managerial staff in different sectors. The VAMNICOM was developed as an apex institute of study and research and the performance of the cooperative movement during this plan period presents a mixed picture of achievements and failures. For example, in the field of marketing the plan targets were exceeded while in the field of storage and credit the targets were achieved substantially and performance was far from satisfactory in consumers cooperative.

The movement has penetrated into many sectors which had been the monopoly of the private sector. Significant among them were industrial cooperatives including weaver's cooperatives, milk cooperatives, processing cooperatives, transport cooperatives and housing cooperatives. The rationalization of the central banks all over the country was also completed and a number of apex institutions were established at the national and state level. Side by side the growth of federations had been witnessed during the plans.

The development of cooperative movement was attracting the politicians and by the end of this plan the entry of politics and politicians was quite visible. Much earlier a warning was alarmed by All India Review Committee (1969) which runs as follows:

> "The experience of the last few years does seem to suggest that there is a real danger of the operational policies and methods of cooperatives being governed by political considerations, though neither the entry of politicians into the ranks of cooperative leadership not the emergence of cooperators as political leaders need by an undesirable development in itself. From the limited point of view of rural credit, it is clear to us that political interest in certain instances, have begun to affect the working of the institutions in various ways, causing credit to be denied to certain groups or to be provided to others in transgression of the rules in force or causing repayment of cooperative dues to be delayed or ignored".[20]

In fact before launching the fifth year plan a tug of war had started between politicians and officials. One wanted the other to surrender and let him along exploit the opportunity. Nehru warned the Nation about exploitation of cooperatives by the vested interests and left behind his clean vision of cooperation.

After Nehru the policy on cooperation remained unchanged during the period of Indira Gandhi but with the passage of time more corruption and political as well as official domination took place. The movement marched ahead with all symptoms of chronic ailment.

Fifth Five Year Plan (April 1, 1974 to March 31, 1979)

In the Fifth Plan, the objective was to consolidate and strengthen the network of agricultural cooperatives in aid of sustained agricultural development, making consumers' cooperatives more viable, correcting regional imbalances, and focusing the activities of the cooperatives more and more on small and marginal farmers and weaker sections of the population.

The building up of a strong and viable cooperative sector, with special emphasis on the needs of the peasants, the workers and consumers, were the major objectives of national policy during the Fifth Plan. The Draft Fifth Five Year Plan (1947-1979) stated:

> "Cooperation is eminently suited to bring about desired socio-economic challenges in the context of the existing conditions in the country. There is no other instrument as potentially powerful and full of social purpose as the cooperative".

Specific Objectives

Four specific objectives had been stated for cooperative development during the Fifth Plan.

(1) To strengthen the network of agricultural cooperatives (credit planning for a process of sustained agricultural development);

(2) To build up a viable consumer cooperative movement to enable it to function as an important element in a consumer oriented distribution system;

(3) To make efforts towards the correction of regional imbalances in the level of cooperative development particularly in the sphere of agricultural credit;

(4) Special efforts will be made towards restructuring and reorienting the cooperatives so as to shift the focus on their activities increasingly in favour of small and marginal farmers and other under-privileged section of the people.[21]

The cooperative movement was regarded as an important instrument for implementing national policies of "Growth with Social Justice". In October 1974, the Department of Civil Supplies and Cooperation was created in the Ministry of Industry and Civil Supplies. The primary objective was to coordinate and assist multi-pronged action on state government levels and the Union ministries to ensure the production and distribution of essential commodities and to combat inflation.

The activities of the Department were geared to implementation of the 20 point economic programme. The Department was specially concerned with (i) measures for price stability, availability and distribution of essential commodities; (ii) supplies of essential commodities to students' hostels in colleges and universities; and (iii) distribution of controlled cloth.

One of the primary objectives of Government Policy during Fifth Plan was not only to increase the production of essential consumer goods, but also to make them available to people at reasonable prices. The strategy adopted for this purpose was two-fold viz., expansion and streamlining of the public distribution of consumer articles. There were nearly 66,000 cooperative retail outlets for distribution of consumer goods in urban and rural areas. One of the major items handled by cooperatives was controlled cloth. Another development during this period has been the extension of cooperative activities to serve the student community in the hostels of universities and degree colleges. Cooperatives are supplying essential consumer goods to about 3,000 hostels covering nearly 2.4 percent students.

To broaden the financial base of consumer cooperatives, the central government provided during 1975-76, special assistance of Rs. 4.55 crores to the State Governments for contributing to the share capital of consumer cooperatives. The National Cooperative Development Corporation has also formulated a scheme for assisting expansion of consumer cooperative activities in rural areas through marketing and service cooperatives.

In the context of a national pattern, which is being evolved, the system of workers' participation in management (WPM) was introduced in large cooperative industrial units. Special cooperative programmes directed to increasing employment and income opportunities to vulnerable sections were evolved implemented. The National Cooperative Development Corporation also extended its activities to cover cooperative programmes for weaker sections.

While the overall progress of cooperative movement appears striking, there were wide regional disparities. The level of development of agricultural cooperatives was not uniform in all states. A number of schemes were evolved with financial assistance from the central government for accelerating the growth of agricultural cooperatives in the cooperatively underdeveloped states.

In order to reduce regional disparities, the following rates of increase in short-term production credit were envisaged in the Fifth Plan:

a. In the advanced states in Group A (Punjab, Kerala, Gujarat, Tamil Nadu and Maharashtra) an increase of about 10 per cent per annum was considered appropriate;

b. For the states in Group B (Andhra Pradesh, Haryana, Himachal Pradesh, Jammu and Kashmir, Karnataka, Madhya Pradesh and Uttar Pradesh) about 15 percent annual rate of growth was considered necessary.

c. For the states in group C (Assam, Bihar, Meghalaya, Orissa, Rajasthan, West Bengal, Manipur, Tripura and Nagaland), it was considered necessary to provide for a growth rate of about 20 per annum.

The SFDA and MFAL projects started functioning on a significant scale only from the cooperative year 1971-72. By the end of March 1975, 87 SFDA and MFAL had identified 19.90 lakh small farmers, 21.46 lakh marginal farmers and 4.68 lakh agricultural labourers; of these 23.28 lakhs were brought within the cooperative fold. During the Fifth Plan, the number of these projects increased to 160, including the existing 87 projects. All the projects were composite, covering small and marginal farmers and agricultural labourers. The parameters for identification of small and marginal farmers had also been reduced to 2.02 hectares of dryland in the case of small farmers and 1.01 hectares of dryland in the case of marginal farmers. In the new projects, the emphasis was on crop husbandry programme which included intensive agricultural, multiple cropping, introduction of high-yielding varieties, development of irrigation, social conservation, land shaping and land development, with special emphasis on dry farming practices and water harvesting measures.

In the field of marketing emphasis was laid on the consolidation and strengthening of existing societies. About 100 new primary marketing societies were to be organized. There societies were expected to handle agricultural produce of Rs. 1900 crores. Moreover, they were expected to step up their operation in the field of exports.

The structure of processing units established in the cooperative sector conforms two distinct, patterns, namely, units established by independent processing societies and units established as adjuncts to cooperative marketing societies. Under the first category fall the larger units such as sugar factories, solvent extraction plans and spinning mills. Medium and small units such as rice mills, oil mills, jute baling units, cotton ginning and pressing units mostly fall under the second category.

The All India Rural Credit Survey Committee recommended for the provisions of arrangements for training of personnel in cooperative department and institution and for education of members and office bearers of societies. However, much attention had not been given as this investment was considered incapable of giving quick results for the window dressing of the balance sheet. However, Fifth Plan intensified the cooperative education and training programmes at all levels. The management of cooperative institutions was considered vital. Suitable measures were taken for the establishment of cadres at appropriate levels in different sectors of the movement.

The main targets of the Fifth Five Year Plan were as follows:

Fifth Plan Cooperative Targets[22]

	Item	*Assured Level 1973-74*	*Base Targeted Level 1978-79*
1.	Short-term advances by Primary agricultural credit societies	700	1300
2.	Medium term advances by primary agricultural credit societies during the five years of the plan	200	325
3.	Long-term advances by the land development banks in five years of the plan period.	900	1500
4.	Value of agricultural produce annually marketed by Cooperatives	1100	1900
5.	Number of cooperative processing units installed by the end of years (nos.)	1500	2150
6.	Value of chemical fertilizers annually retailed by Cooperatives	350	380
7.	Capacity of cooperative storage at the end of the year	33 lakh tonnes	68 lakh tonnes
8.	Value of consumer goods annually retailed by urban consumer cooperatives	300	600

Based on the 13 recommendations of an Expert Group appointed by the Planning Commission in 1972, structural reform of the cooperative setup was envisaged. The Plan recommended the formulation of Farmers' Services Cooperative Societies as had been envisaged by the National Commission on Agriculture and stressed the need for professional management of cooperatives.

Sixth Five Year Plan (April 1, 1980 to 31 March, 1955)

The then government ended the Fifth Five Year Plan, one year earlier to its term i.e, only within four yeas span (1974-78) and introduced a new plan since April 1, 1978. This plan was named as the "Rolling Plan". In the first phase of this Rolling Plan, the Sixth Plan was initially started for 5 years (1978-83) on April 1, 1978. In 1980, the Sixth Plan (Rolling Plan) prepared by the Janata Government was abandoned by the Congress Government and a new Sixth Plan was introduced for the period 1980-1985.

In the light of the problems faced during the fifth plan this plan proposed to direct attention on the following:

1. A clearly conceived action programme was drawn up for strengthening of primary village societies so that they are able to effectively act as multi-purpose units catering to diverse needs of their members;
2. Existing cooperation policies and procedures were examined with a view to ensuring that the efforts of the cooperative are more systematically directed towards ameliorating the economic condition of the rural poor;
3. Re-orientation and consolidation of the role of the cooperative federal organization viewed necessary so that they may be able through their constituent organizations to effectively support a rapidly diversifying and expanding agricultural sector, including horticulture, food processing, poultry, dairying, fishery, animal husbandry, sericulture etc., with credit, input supply, marketing and other services.

The total central plan outlay for various schemes for the sixth plan period was Rs. 330.15 crores. The outlay in the state and union territories sector was Rs. 584.08 crores. Thus, total public sector outlay on various schemes of cooperation was Rs. 914.23 crores.[23]

There were some special programmes of rural development like RDP, DPAR, DDP, National Grid of Rural godowns in which cooperatives were assigned an active role. Other programmes like cooperative training as education etc., are directly concerned with the cooperation sector.

The public sector outlay on cooperation during sixth plan was as follows:[24]

Cooperative Credit	85.00
Cooperative Marketing Processing and Storage	178.50
Consumer cooperative	10.50
Miscellaneous	0.15

In 1981 the NABARD was set up to provide refinance support to Cooperative Banks and to supplement the resources of Commercial Banks and Regional Rural Banks to enhance credit flow to the agriculture and rural sector. Also the Multi-Unit Cooperative Societies Act of 1942 was repealed and Multi State Cooperative Societies Act of 1984 was enacted.

In 1982 a new 20 Point Programme was announced by the Prime Minister. About 14 programmes were directly concerned with the cooperation.

The National Cooperative Union of India as the chief spokesman of the Indian Cooperative Movement prepared following action programme for the adoption by the cooperatives throughout the country.

a) Creating awareness among members and public;

b) Convening meetings/conference/seminars workshops to widely discuss the programme.

c) Taking steps for improving organizational productivity;

d) Organizing irrigation cooperatives for harnessing irrigation potential;

e) Encouraging farmer members to produce more of pulses and oilseeds;

f) Adopting villages for integrated rural development;

g) Improving organizational serviceability for providing credit and other inputs to farmers particularly small and marginal farmers, artisans, handicrafts, handloom weavers, etc.

h) Organizing cooperative farming societies on surplus land released through ceilings;

i) Impressing on farmer members to pay minimum wages to agricultural labourers employed by them;

j) Organizing labour contract cooperative societies for the bonded labour;

k) Organizing and strengthening LAMPS in tribal areas and cooperatives for scheduled castes;

l) Developing drinking water facilities in the villages out of the utilization of common good fund;

m) Organizing housing cooperatives both in rural and urban areas particularly for the economically weak;

n) Organizing and strengthening rural electricity cooperatives;

o) Impressing members to undertake afforestation, social and farm forestry;

p) Advancing loans for setting up biogas plants;

q) Educating members in planned parenthood population, education and family welfare;

r) Organizing cooperative hospitals;

s) Strengthening women education programme particularly in regard to child welfare, maternity, nutrition, balanced diet, etc.

t) Organizing adult education and literacy programmes;

u) Involving village and consumer cooperatives in distribution of essential commodities;

v) Simplifying procedures for availing of financial and other assistance;

w) Organizing campaigns for domestic savings.

Various cooperative organizations in the country have undertaken a number of steps to prepare their own action programme suiting to the local situations. Special programmes of rural development, community development and Panchayati Raj and Cooperation in States, Union Territories were also encouraged.

Targets for Cooperative Operations

Physical Programmes	*Anticipated Achievement 1979-80*	*Target for 1984-85*
Shot-term Loans	Rs. 1300 crores	Rs. 2500 crores
Medium-term Loans	Rs. 125 crores	Rs. 240 crores
Long-term Loans	Rs. 275 crores	Rs. 555 crores
Agricultural Products Marketed through Cooperatives	Rs. 170 crores	Rs. 2500
Fertilizer to be distributed through cooperatives Quantity Value	23.50 Lakh Tonnes (NPK) Rs. 900 crores	45 Lakh Tonnes (NPK) Rs. 1600 crores
Consumer goods to be distributed through cooperatives in rural areas in urban areas	Rs. 800 crores 800 crores	Rs. 2000 crores Rs. 1600 crores

Source: Mathur, B.S., *Cooperation in India*, Sahtiya Bhawan, Agra, 1995,

During this plan the agriculture was expected to grow at an annual compound rates of about 5 percent which needs substantial credit farm inputs and marketing and storage support within this overall growth rate, the rate of growth of production in dairying, animal husbandry, poultry, fishery and fruits and vegetables has been projected at a rate higher than for crops. The rural integrated programme which is expected to cover the entire country also needs multi-typed support from cooperatives. Taking into consideration the demand for cooperative services and the reasonable capabilities of the cooperative system the targets of physical performance in important cooperative activities were projects as follows for the period 1980-85.

The total Central Plan outlay for various schemes of cooperation for the Sixth Plan Period (1980-85) was Rs. 330.15 crores. The outlay in the states and Union Territories was Rs. 584.08 crores. Thus, total public sector outlay on various schemes of cooperation was Rs. 914.23 crores.

A major development in the field of credit during the VI plan period was the setting up of National Bank for Agriculture and Rural Development (NABARD) in July 1982. Now it has emerged as an apex institution accredited with all matters concerning policy, planning and operations in the field of credit and other economic activities in rural areas.

This plan had laid great emphasis on the development and professional manpower and appropriate cadres to man the managerial posts, and for this purpose, recommended intensification of cooperative education and training programmes and their increased linkages to the growing and diversified needs of various sectors of the cooperative movement 5,165 senior level personnel and 38,137 intermediate personnel received training in the Vaikunth Mehta National Institute of Cooperative Management and 17 cooperative training institutions. Too much dependence on Government funds has been a major constraint in the expansion of cooperative training education programmes. Also, evaluation of the training programmes has not been given due attention.

In short, the progress made under various cooperative programmes during the Sixth Plan period presents a mixed picture. Although quantitatively substantial progress has been made under the various programmes and the targets laid down in the Plan were more or less achieved. A number of shortcomings have also been noticed in the implementation of these programmes. In spite of the sizeable assistance provided to the cooperatively weaker states particularly in the north eastern region, the cooperative movement in these states has not yet picked up. By far the most serious lacuna has been the continued existence of high levels of overdues in a large number of states which has eroded the overall viability of primary cooperatives and has also adversely affected other fields of activity like marketing of agricultural produce, supply of agricultural inputs and distribution of goods.[25]

The role of politics, politicians and officials has increased and cooperatives have been labeled as corrupt organizations headed by corrupt personnel and controlled by vested interests. A clear tug of war has been between politicians and bureaucracy and a possible solution was to gradually reduce the influence of these so called cooperative leaders. However, the bureaucracy has turned it into its favour by claiming as professionalized cadre and seeking appointment on deputation as specialist.

Seventh Five Year Plan (April 1, 1985 to March 31, 1990)

This plan pointed out that while there had been all round progress in credit, poor recovery of loans and high level of overdues were matters of concern. The Plan recommended amongst others development of Primary Agricultural Credit Societies as multiple viable units; realignment of policies and procedures to expand flow of credit and ensure inputs and services particularly to weaker sections; special programmes for the North Eastern Region; strengthening of consumer cooperative movement in urban as well as rural areas and promoting professional management.

The targets of cooperative programme in the Seventh Five Year Plan are indicated in the table given below:

Targets of Cooperative Programmes of Seventh Five Year Plan

S.No.	*Programme*	*UnitsRs.*	*Base Level 1984-85*	*Plan Targets 1989-90*
1.	Short-term loans	Crores	2500	5540
2.	Medium-term loans	Crores	250	500
3.	Long-term loans	Crores	500	1030
4.	Value of agricultural produce marketed through cooperative	Crores	2700	5000
5.	Retail sale of fertilizers through cooperatives:			
	a. Quantity	Million tonnes		
	b. Value	Crores	3.631500	8.333400
6	Value of consumer goods distributed in rural areas	Crores	1400	3500
7.	Retail sale of consumer goods by urban consumer cooperatives	Crores	1400	3500
8.	Capacity of cooperative godowns constructed	Million tones	8.00	10.00
9.	Cooperative sugar factories to be installed	Nos.	185	220
10.	Cooperative spinning mills installed	Nos.	90	130
11.	Cold storage to be installed	Nos.	185	250

Source: Seventh Five Year Plan

The seventh plan emphasized policies and programmes, which aimed at rapid growth in food grains production, increased employment opportunities and productivity within the framework of basic tenets of planning, namely, growth modernization, self help and social justice.

Cooperative development under the Seventh Plan embodied the following main tasks:

1. Comprehensive development of primary agricultural credit societies to function as multi-purpose viable units;
2. Realignment of the policies and procedures of cooperatives to expand the flow of credit and ensure supply of inputs and services particularly to the weaker sections;
3. Taking up of special cooperative programmes for implementation in the underdeveloped states specially in the North Eastern Region.
4. Strengthening the consumer cooperative movement in the urban as well as rural areas so that it could play a pivotal role in the public distribution system; and

Promoting professional management and strengthening of effective training facilities for improving the operational efficiency.

The major thrust during the plan was to ensure adequate flow of credit to the weaker sections of the population and to the less developed areas.

During the seventh plan, disbursement of agriculture credit through cooperatives, commercial and regional rural banks increased from Rs. 5,810 crores in 1984-85 to Rs. 12,570 crores by 1989-90. The expansion in short-term, medium and long-term loans through cooperatives picked up only in the fourth year of the seventh plan. The debt relief scheme, announced in 1990-91, affected the recovery climate resulting in a lower volume of credit flow. Several measures were also initiated by NABARD to increase the credit flow. Separate lines of credit for oilseed growers were opened.[26]

For improving the recovery climate and reduction of overdues, greater stress had been laid on the supervision over proper utilization of the loans provision of extension services.

There were 76,000 fertilizer retailer outlets and 40 lakh tonnes of fertilizer nutrients were distributed during 1989-90. The National Agriculture Cooperative Marketing Federation (NAFED) undertook price support operations in respect of oilseeds, coarse grains, pulses, potatoes and onions. The National Agriculture Cooperative Marketing Federation exported 3,36,220 tonnes onion during 1989-90 which helped maintain the price line in domestic market. The NAFED also procured 6,022 tonnes of copra as price support operation.

Cooperative godowns/warehousing capacity increased from 80 lakh tonnes in 1984-85 to 100 lakh tonnes by 1987-88. By 1990-91, 141 lakh tonnes of storage capacity had been created mainly in Punjab, U.P., Maharashtra, M.P., Karnataka, Andhra Pradesh and Himachal Pradesh.

A storage capacity of 114.47 lakh tonnes was also completed under the cooperative sector by 1989-90. In doing so, the Seventh Plan target for creation of additional capacity of 20 lakh tonnes had been exceeded by constructing storage capacity of 35.18 lakh tonnes. The NCDC promoted 239 cold storage units capacity of 6.83 lakh tonnes of which 229 cold storages with 6.35 lakh tonnes capacity were installed. The capacity utilization of the cold storages ranged between 80 and 100 per cent.

It was proposed to increase the number of department stores from 330 at the end of the sixth plan to 430 by the end of the seventh plan. In addition, it was proposed to increase the number of retail outlets of consumer stores from 31960 to 32660 by training and education programmes. The capacity of the Vaikunth Mehta National Institute of Cooperative Management was proposed to be increased from 5000 to 6000 in the Seventh Plan. Similarly, the training output of cooperative colleges was to be increased to 51800 and the number of junior cooperative training centres was proposed to be raised from 83 to 150 by the end of the Seventh Plan.[27]

However, the main emphasis was on the use of capabilities of cooperatives in the achievement of targets in the field of credit, marketing, processing, storage and consumer cooperative as this could not have been done by any other agency. As cooperative education, training and management were vital for achieving targets in the above segments of cooperative sector, therefore, programmes related to them were intensified. Development and strengthening of cooperative sector was not the aim nor the plan made any commitment, as it did earlier about utility and desirability of the cooperative sector and its role in Indian economy.

With increasing demand from proponents of an autonomous cooperative movement and reforms in the Cooperative laws, the Government constituted a Committee on Cooperative Law for Democratization and Professionalization of Management in Cooperatives in 1985, headed by Shri K.N. Ardhanareeswaran. The Committee recommended the deletion of those legal provisions in State Cooperative Acts, which militate against the democratic character and autonomy of cooperatives, and also recommended incorporation of several provisions which could activize democratic processes for infusing professional management into cooperatives.

Similarly, in 1989 the Agricultural Credit Review Committee under the chairmanship of Prof. A.M. Khusro examined the problems of agricultural and rural credit and recommended a major systematic improvement. The Committee recommended that the Eighth Plan should become the plan for revival of weak agricultural credit societies.

Eighth Five Year Plan (April 1, 1992 to March 31, 1997)

The VIII five year plan which was supposed to start from April 1, 1990 could not be started on scheduled time because of some political changes at the Centre during 1990-92. The National Development Council ratified the format of the plan in one of its meeting held on May 23, 1992. This plan began on April 1, 1992 which ended on March 31, 1997.

The plan 1992-97 laid emphasis on building up the cooperative movement as a self-managed, self-regulated and self-reliant institutional setup, by giving it more autonomy and democratizing the movement. It also spoke of enhancing the capability of cooperatives for improving economic activity and creating employment opportunities for small farmers, labourers, artisans, scheduled castes, scheduled tribes and women and emphasized development and training of cooperative functionaries in professional management.

It was launched immediately after the initiation of structural adjustment policies and macro stabilization policies, which were necessitated by the worsening Balance of Payments position and inflation during 1990-91. The various structural adjustment policies were introduced gradually so that the economy could be pushed to a higher growth path and improve its strength and thus prevent Balance of Payments and inflation crisis in future. The Plan took note of some of these policy changes, which were to come about due to these reforms.[28]

1. Open door market economy in which imports and exports are liberalized facilitating free trade of goods and services.
2. Privatization of public sector enterprises on a selective basis and removing all entry restrictions so that multinationals can also set up their industries in India to bring in new technologies and to increase competitiveness.
3. New banking policy in which interest rates would be determined by market forces and withdrawing restrictions on lending to priority sector except in the case of small and marginal farmers.
4. Withdrawal of Government patronage in the form of curtailing subsidies, concessions and grant-in-aids with a view

to encourage Indian industry to become self-reliant and professionally managed.

The main approach of the new economic environment was liberalization or de-regulation, privatization and marketisation. Precisely speaking, liberalization or de-regulation means withdrawal or removal of restrictive and regulative measures, imposed by the Government through licensing system and various other controlling measures. Privatization means expansion of private sector and minimization of the role of public sector or government undertakings. Marketisation implies, by and large, no Government intervention and interference in the market by way of regulating market situation, enforcing administered prices, quotas etc. and thus leaving the market forces to have a free play of demand and supply. The globalization means to open the national market by removing or minimizing restriction.

Cooperatives have flourished and strengthened under capitalism as well as socialism. They had record success under socialist pattern of society provided a level playing field is given to them. Today they work under state government and follow the restrictions imposed by the state laws. Also the banking units work side by side under Reserve Bank of India and follow the rules and regulations imposed by the RBI as well as NABARD without enjoying the benefits granted to other banks whom they compete in the market. The companies working under company law are not so heavily burdened as the cooperatives are. Lack of clear policy perception at the level of government in regard to the place of cooperatives under the new economic policies as it has been in case of public and private sectors is one of the reasons for the cold attitude of the government.

Till Sixth Five Year Plan, there used to be a specific chapter defining the policy perspective for cooperative development in every plan document. However, since the Seventh Five Year Plan a specific chapter on cooperation did not find place in the Plan Document. In 1990, an Expert Committee, under the chairmanship of Choudhary Brahm Prakash, was appointed by the Planning Commission to make a rapid review of the broad status of the cooperative movement, suggest future directions and finalize a Model Cooperatives Act. The Committee submitted its report in 1991. Since cooperation is a state subject and each state has its own cooperative legislation covering cooperatives whose membership is confined to the state, the report of the Committee, along with a draft Model Cooperative Law, was circulated to all State Governments for their consideration and adoption at State level. The 8th and 9th Five Year Plans document contains a sketchy programme of cooperatives under Agriculture and Allied activities. From the *Ninth Plan (1997-2002)* onwards, there has been no specific mention about cooperatives as a part of the Plan.

While the initial intentions as per the first few plans seemed to promote the sector with all possible assistance and benevolence from the government, the later plans clearly show the clouding of this perception. By the Seventh Plan, the idea that cooperatives are mere instrumental in the lands of the government to implement its developmental and populist measures, had become an unquestioned assumption. The allocations of budget, the determining of focus and the target implementation approach had all furthered this approach, by then, the government, had seen what the cooperatives could do for the government rather than what could be done for the cooperatives.

The thirteenth Indian Cooperative Congress (1997) the highest forum of Indian Cooperative Movement drew attention of the Government to this important policy deviation regarding cooperatives and unanimously requested the government of India to recognize "Cooperation" as a specific sector of Indian economy as it has been done in case of private and public sectors but nothing was done.

The strategy for cooperative credit development in the Eighth Plan was as follows:

(i) Building up the cooperative movement as a self managed, self regulated and self reliant institutional set-up by giving more autonomy to cooperatives and by democratizing the movement;

(ii) Enhancing the capabilities of cooperative for enabling them to play a significant role in improving the productivity of the economy and in creating employment opportunities for the people living in rural areas for service of weaker sections viz., small farmers, labourer, workers, artisans, the scheduled castes scheduled tribes and women;

(iii) Strengthening cooperative credit and organize structure in accordance with model laws and to make it competitive and viable;

(iv) Extend adequate credit support to the programmes of national priority and poverty alleviation such as the special rice/ Foodgrains Production Programme, National Oilseeds Development Programme, Oilseeds Production Thrust Programme, etc. larger flow of funds for thrust areas i.e., to dryland areas, minor irrigation, and wastelands development through non-farm sector activities could be considered on priority.

(v) Appropriate linking of consumer cooperatives for implementing Public Distribution System for the benefit and protection of consumers interest was to be ensured.

(vi) Development and training of cooperative functionaries in professional management and introduction of suitable personnel management policy to meet the demand for professional managerial personnel in the cooperatives;

(vii) Review of cooperatives with a view to liberalize the working of cooperative institutions and freeing them from bureaucratic control.

S.No.	*Programme*	*Base Level 1991-92 Anticipated Achievement*	*Eighth Plan Targets 1996-97*
1.	Short term loans (Rs. Crores)	4350	7050
2.	Medium term loans (Rs. Crores)	360	615
3.	Long term Loans	965	1625
4.	Cooperative Marketing of agricultural produce (Rs. Crores)	7130	9500
5.	Value of Fertilisers retailed by Coops. (Rs. Corres)	2475	4000
6.	Value of consumer goods distributed in rural area (Rs. Crores)	2725	4500
7.	Value of consumer goods distributed in urban area (Rs. Crores)	2700	5000
8.	Coop. Sugar factories installed (NO.s)	220	269
9.	Coop. Spinning Mills installed (No.)	130	158
10.	Capacity of coop. godowns constructed (lakh tonnes)	121	142
11.	Cold storages (No.)	39	309

Source: Eighth Five Year Plan, p. 20.

One of the major issues concerning the cooperative sector was the professionalisation of management. If the cooperatives have to compete in a more open economic regime, the state Governments will have to professionalise the management of cooperatives. This is crucial for overall cooperative development vis-à-vis other sectors. For achieving this, it was considered necessary to convince the State Government of the need for granting functional autonomy to cooperatives.

The Plan had mentioned that the growth of cooperatives sector had not been uniform in all parts of the country. The primary reasons for this situation were control of cooperatives by document vested interest groups, poor management, dependence of cooperatives of higher tiers and government for financial assistance and limited range of business activities. The function of thrift had not been given due importance by cooperatives leading to resource crunch and ultimately to their inability to serve the poor. The Agriculture Credit Review Committee (ACRC) and the committee for implementation of recommendation of ACRC stressed on a programme of business development planning in respect of each PACs with a view to diversifying loan operations, generation of internal resources through deposit mobilization and enlarging package of profitable non-credit services. The working group on promotion of Self-Help Groups as sub-system in Primary Agricultural Cooperatives had made important recommendation relating to the improvement of functioning of cooperatives. There is a need to strengthen the resource base of PACS to enable the group members to undertake investments necessary for expanding their production levels.[29]

Further, it was stated that cooperatives have, over the years, significantly diversified their activities to include credit, banking, input distribution, agro processing, storage and warehousing. In dairying and oil processing activities, cooperative sub-sector has emerged as an important counterveiling factor to the private traders, for the benefit to both producers and consumers.

Ninth Five Year Plan (April 1, 1997 to March 31, 2002)

The introduction of market economy from 1991 has changed the entire strategy and concept of our economic development. The Nehruvian period ended much earlier new thinking started. A parliamentarian forum came into existence to back up the agenda of the NCUI and seek help of the government for cooperatives as per agenda of the NCUI. But nothing substantial has so far been achieved, not even a chapter in the plan document, no level playing field for cooperatives, no declaration of government policy on cooperation, no approval of the IBC. Cooperatives were earlier flattered, later on controlled and now dictated by politicians, ministers. bureaucrats, M.Ps'. and their miniatures at local level.[30]

With this background the cooperatives have entered into the era of free economy. Although the NCUI claims to be the champion of the cause of cooperative movement but in practice it has nurtured the policy of patronizing political bosses. The ninth five year plan 1997-2001, was launched. Memorandum of the NCUI and many recommendations of committees appointed from time to time were placed before the governments, for boosting up cooperatives by remedying the deficiencies, defects and lacunas in the organization and working of this sector. The ninth plan again omitted the chapter on cooperation. It has made some reference of the cooperatives and recognized their role in the agricultural development and allied activities. Perhaps the government has not seriously studied the implications of its policy regarding cooperative sector which is as important as public and private sector.

The Ninth Plan accorded priority to agriculture and rural development with a view to generating adequate productive employment and eradication of poverty, accelerating the growth rate of the economy with stable prices; ensuring food and nutritional security for all, particularly the vulnerable sections of the society, providing the basic minimum services of safe drinking water, primary health care facilities, universal primary education, shelter, and connectivity to all in a time bound manner; containing the growth rate of population ensuring environment sustainability of the development process through social mobilization and participation of people at all levels, empowerment of women as socially disadvantaged groups such as Scheduled Caste, Scheduled Tribes and Other Backward Classes and Minorities as agents of socio-economic change and development, promoting and developing people's participatory bodies like Panchayati Raj Institutions, cooperatives and self-help groups; and strengthening efforts to build self-reliance.

From the early days to planning cooperatives have been perceived as the most important form of people's institutions for promotion of equity, social justice and economic development. Every effort will be made to make the cooperatives work. They need to be liberated from tight bureaucratic control. Self-help Groups, Associations of Workers or Small Producers, etc. are other forms of institutions which will be encouraged. Government will seek active partnership with the voluntary sector in organizing and promoting these institutions.

In short the Ninth Plan (1997-2002) has not determined any target to be achieved by this sector in its various segments. It gave only sketchy account of credit, marketing fertilizer, fisheries etc. and did not assign any specific role in the economy of the country. Cooperatives have equally developed under capitalism, socialism and monarchy provided they are helped equally. In the USA, for example, cooperatives annually account for 70% of fluid milk, 35% of agricultural credit of all types of green oilseeds, substantial share in rural electrification-production, transmission and distribution of bulk of fertilizers. In Japan, cooperatives are fairly strong to influence the market in the field of agricultural marketing, fisheries, forestry and distributive consumers trade. There are 110 university cooperative stores very strong and effective. The Scandinavian countries have a very vast network of cooperatives. The erstwhile communist bloc countries, where the economy is in transition, the cooperatives are being reorganized to continue playing as partner in developing and change.[31]

In India the cooperative movement is at cross-road and has been passing through a critical phase. It would be advisable to restructure the whole cooperative movement. The Government should constitute a commission on cooperation to examine the various aspects including the shortfalls in the Cooperative Movement and to propose an effective programme of action for the future.[32]

REFERENCES

13. Government of India, Planning Commission, *First Five Year Plan, Cooperative Sector in India*, S. Chand & Sons, New Delhi.

14. *All India Rural Credit Survey*, Vol. II, p. 376.

15. Government of India Planning Commission, Second Five Year Plan 1956-57 to 1960-61.

16. Sharma B.D. and Manchanda Anita, "Jawaharlal Nehru and Indira Gandhi on Cooperation (NCUI), National Cooperative Printing Press, New Delhi.

17. Mathur, B. S., *Cooperation in India*, Sahitya Bhawan, Agra, 1995, p. 76.

18. Hajela, T. N. *Cooperative During the Planning Era*, p. 99.

19. Based on Press Summary released by the R. B. of India on 30th July 1969, Quoted from T. N. Hajela Cooperation in India, p. 103.

20. T. N. Hejela, *Cooperative during the Planning Era*, p. 111.

21. Mathur, B. S. *Cooperation of India*, Sahitya Bhawan, Agra, p. 81 see fifth five year plan for details.

22. Mathur, B. S. *Cooperation of India*, Sahitya Bhawan, Agra, p. 82.

23. Planning Commission, *Sixth Five Year Plan*, 1980-85, p. 177.

24. *Ibid.*, p. 177.

25. Government of India, Planning Commission, *Seventh Five Year Plan 1985-90*, Vol. 2, p. 25.

26. Planning Commission, *Eighth Five Year Plan*, p.4

27. Mathur, B. S., *Cooperation in India*, Sahitya Bhavan, Agra, 1995

28. Government of India, *Eighth Five Year Plan*, p. 356.

29. *Ibid.* p. 18

30. *Ninth Five Year Plan, 1997-2000*, Vol. I, Nabhi Publications, p.1.

31. Dwivedi, R. C., New Economic Environment and Cooperative Identity, NCUI, Souvenir 13th Indian Cooperative Congress, 21-22 January, 1997, New Delhi, p. 56.

32. Mohan Dharia, Challenges before the Cooperative Development and Role of Voluntary Organizations, NCUI: Souvenir 13th Indian Cooperative Congress 21-22 January 1997, New Delhi, p.53.

3

Post-Liberalization Developments

Model Cooperatives Act, 1990

The government appointed an Expert Committee in 1990 under the chairmanship of Choudhary Brahm Prakash, to make a rapid review of the broad status of the cooperative movement, suggest future directions and finalize a Model Cooperatives Act. The Committee submitted its report in 1991. Since cooperation is a state subject and each state has its own cooperative legislation covering cooperatives whose membership is confined to the state, the report of the Committee, along with a draft Model Cooperative Law, was circulated to all State Governments for their consideration and adoption at state level. (See Appendix)

National Policy on Cooperative (2002)

In 2002, the Government of India enunciated a National Cooperative Policy. The objective of the Policy is to facilitate an all round development of cooperatives in the country. The policy promises to provide cooperatives with the necessary support, encouragement and assistance, to ensure their functioning as autonomous, self-reliant and democratically managed institutions, accountable to their members, and making a significant contribution to the national economy.

The National Policy on Cooperatives would seek to achieve:

- Ensuring functioning of the cooperatives based on basic cooperative values and principles as enshrined in the Declaration of the International Cooperative Alliance Congress, 1995;
- Revitalization of the cooperative structure, particularly in the sector of agricultural credit;
- Reduction of regional imbalances through provision of support measures by the Central Government/State Governments, particularly in the underdeveloped and cooperatively undeveloped States/regions.
- Strengthening of the Cooperative Education and Training and Human Resource Development for professionalization of the management of the cooperatives;
- Greater participation of members in the management of cooperatives and promoting the concept of user members;
- Amendment/Removal of provisions in cooperative laws providing for the restrictive regulatory regime;
- Evolving a system of integrated cooperative structure by entrusting the federations predominantly the role of promotion, guidance, information system, etc. towards their affiliate members and potential members;
- Evolving a system of in-built mechanism in Cooperative legislation to ensure timely conduct of general body meetings, elections and audit of cooperative societies;
- Ensuring that the benefits of the cooperatives' endeavour reach the poorer sections of the society and encouraging the participation of such sections and women in management of cooperatives. (See Annexure)

Multi-State Cooperative Societies Act, 2002

The Multi-State Cooperative Societies (MSCS) Act, enacted in 1984, was modified in 2002, in keeping with the spirit of the Model Cooperatives Act. Unlike the state laws, which remained as a parallel legislation to co-exist with the earlier laws, the MSCS Act, 2002 replaced the earlier Act of 1984. (See Annexure)

The Multi-State Cooperative Societies (Amendment) Bill, 2010 was introduced in the Lok Sabha recently. The Bill proposes to amend the Multi-State Cooperative Society Act, 2002 in view of the recommendations made by a High Power Committee on cooperation and suggestions received from the different sectors of the cooperative movement and other stakeholders. It has been the demand of the cooperative movement to provide a level playing field to the cooperative sector by removing the restrictive features for the existing cooperative law but it is regret to note that the proposed bill carries many restrictive provisions adversely affecting the autonomy and independence of the cooperatives which will be detrimental for the growth and the development of the cooperatives. The government should create an atmosphere an atmosphere which is more liberal and enabling for the cooperatives to grow, perform and participate in diversified activities. We all know that cooperatives are run by the members themselves who are responsible to meet their common goal with a chance to succeed and risk to fail. More control by the government is detrimental and ineffective and does more harms than help. Need of the hour is to create a sense of responsibility among members depending less on government and becoming more financially self-reliant. This will a more professional approach with commitment and responsibility.

In the proposed bill for the redemption of share the society may refund in full or part of the share capital held by the government on the face value or the back value of the share which is higher. It may be noted that this is not in tune with the cooperative principle which do not differentiate between the government and the normal members. Whereas the proposed provision envisages refund to the government on face value or book value. It is not same in case of non-government member. We cannot have two different standards or parameters. This will lead to legal complications and this matter needs to be further elaborated in the proposed amendment and can't be accepted in the present form. Similarly, the creation of Cooperative Election Authority (CEA) is a welcome one but the election rules to be finalized early. It is for the consideration whether the cooperative election authority can function as a part of Election Commission of India or not and who will bear the cost of the election of loss making societies. Similarly, in case of disposable of net profit, government proposes to establish a cooperative rehabilitation and reconstruction fund in which Multi-State Cooperative Societies contribute on turnover basis subject to maximum of Rs. 3 crore per year and instead of turnover it should be based on net profit of the Multi-State Cooperative Societies.

It will be in the interest of the cooperative movement to place this bill before the standing committee on agriculture to have further healthy discussion and improvement of the proposed bill from its present form. It is very unfortunate that cooperatives are unnecessarily regulated other than by the Annual General Body which is supreme in the affair of cooperative society. Unnecessary control creates more problem and unhealthy dependence on the government. The ideal situation would be maintaining the relationship between the cooperative and the government based on national cooperative policy which is developed to promote the sector without interference.[33]

With the objective of introducing a comprehensive central legislation to facilitate the organization and functioning of genuine multi-state societies and to bring uniformity in their administration and management, the MSCS Act of 1984 was enacted. The earlier Multi-Unit Cooperative Societies Act of 1942 was repealed.

Parallel Cooperative Legislation

As discussed earlier from the *Ninth Plan* onwards, cooperatives have not been given specific place in the plan. Since Cooperation is a State subject and recognizing the difficulties in having the existing State Cooperative Acts amended on the lines of the Model Cooperatives Act, a section of cooperators and civil society initiated action to put in place Parallel Cooperative Legislation for self-reliant cooperatives. Self-reliant cooperatives may be defined as those which have not received any assistance from the Government in the form of equity contribution, loans and guarantees. These Acts are largely based on the recommendations of the Choudhary Brahm Prakash Committee. Nine States namely AP (1995), MP (1999), Bihar (1996), J&K (1999), Orissa (2001), Karnataka (1997), Jharkhand (1996)), Chhattisgarh (1999) and Uttarakhand (2003), have so far enacted Parallel Cooperative Acts which are enabling and ensure autonomous and democratic functioning of cooperatives.[34]

The Companies Amendment Act, 2002

A Committee under the chairmanship of Dr.Y.K. Alagh recommended the amendment of the Companies Act, 1956. On the basis of the recommendations of the Committee, the Producer Companies Bill was introduced in the Parliament and became law on *6th February, 2003 as Part IXA - Producer Companies in the Companies Act, 1956*. Based on the cooperative principles of mutual assistance, it provides an alternative to the institutional form that is presently available to cooperative enterprises.

Producers Cooperatives

In view of the fact that the cooperatives cannot sustain in a competitive market. The Indian Companies Act 1956 has been amended by inserting a specific part IX-A for incorporating producers companies which are expected to operate on cooperative principles of mutual assistance and patronage. Operationally, they would enjoy the same freedom as other private Companies enjoy. For protecting them from takeovers, their shares can not be tradeable at the stock exchange and membership is restricted to primary producers.

Management of producers company can be conducted by an elected Board of Directors who shall enjoy defined tenure of maximum 5 years. However, appointment of Chief Executive shall be mandatory of each Company. The producer company having turn over of Rs. 5 crores and above shall have whole time Secretary who should be member of Institute of Company Secretaries in India.[35]

NCDC Amendment Act, 2002

The origin of NCDC goes back to the recommendations of All India Rural Credit Survey Committee 1954. After a long consideration the NCDC Act was passed in 1963. The main functions of NCDC are to plan, promote and finance programmes of processing, storage and marketing of agricultural produce as also distribution of agricultural produce as also distribution of agricultural inputs and supply of consumer goods. In the non-farm sector, the Corporation's endeavour is to equip cooperatives with facilities to promote income generating streams of activities for the rural poor; such as poultry, dairy, fishery, sericulture, handlooms etc. besides taking up programmes for economic uplift of scheduled castes and scheduled tribes. The NCDC over the years has thus emerged as a developmental financing institution for cooperatives in these sectors.

The Corporation's financial assistance is not individual beneficiary oriented but is meant for institutional development of cooperatives to create common facilities like godowns, processing units and other income generating assets as also to equip them with equity and margin money for raising bank credit and thus provide services to their members.

The Corporation's activities extend to agricultural produce, foodstuffs, minor forest produce and notified commodities i.e.

commodities with respect to which Parliament has legislative powers by virtue of entry 33 in the VII Schedule to the Constitution of India. Some of the commodities notified for the purpose of the NCDC Act are fertilizers, insecticides, agricultural machinery, lac, soap, kerosene oil, textiles, rubber etc.[36]

Recognizing the need to improve its scope of lending and to bring about changes in its funding, the NCDC Act was amended in 2002, which has enabled it to cover notified services, livestock and industrial activities and more importantly to directly fund cooperatives against suitable security.

In accordance with the recommendation made at a Conference of State Ministers for Cooperation, the Government of India in 2002 constituted a Ministerial Task Force to formulate a plan of action for implementation of National Cooperative Policy. The Task Force suggested that a single law instead of parallel laws should be introduced in the states. It also recommended, among others, that in order to depoliticize cooperatives, Members of Parliament or Members of Legislative Assemblies should not be allowed to hold office of any cooperative society.

Also the NCDC Act was amended in 2002 to enable it to cover notified services livestock and industrial activities and more importantly to directly fund cooperatives against suitable security.[*]

Task Force on Revival of Cooperative Credit Institutions

In 2004 the hundredth year of cooperative movement the Government of India in August 2004 set up a Task Force to suggest an action plan for reviving rural cooperative credit institutions and legal measures necessary for facilitating this process. The Task Force, chaired by Prof. A. Vaidyanathan, recommended that any financial

[*] For details see authors book, National Cooperative Development Corporation: *A Critical Study of its Genesis, Organization, Management, Finances and Functioning* AMU Press.

restructuring which did not address the root causes of the weaknesses of the system would not result in its sustained revival and would require legal measures. The recommendations of the Task Force in accordance with its terms of reference are basically confined to revival of credit cooperatives for which it suggests a financial package. The Vaidyanathan Committee has also suggested a model cooperative law that can be enacted by the State Governments. Recommendations of the Task Force are being currently implemented. The Vaidyanathan Committee has also given its report on the long-term cooperative credit structure.

Today cooperatives cover approximately 99% of Indian villages and 71% of total rural households in the country. Their contribution to the national economy may be seen from the following table.

Cooperative share in the economy

	Percentage
Agricultural Credit Disbursed	18*
Fertilizer Distributed	36*
Production of Fertilizer	25*
Sugar Produced	50**
Spindleage	10#
Milk Procurement to total Production	8$
Yarn Production	22#
Handlooms	54#
Wheat Procurement	33#
Fishermen Cooperatives	21#
Storage Facilities (Village Level PACS)	64#

Source:

*	DOAC, Government of India (2009)
**	National Federation of Sugar Cooperatives (2009)
#	NCUI Profile (2006)
$	Department of AHD&F, Government of India.

NOTES

33. *The Cooperator* 2010, Editorial, p. 262.
34. For details see B.D. Sharma, *Cooperative Legislation : From State Control to autonomy and independence, Hundred Years of Cooperative Development,* NCUI, 2007.
35. *Hundred Years of Cooperative Development in India*, National Cooperative Union of India, 3, Siri Institutional Area, August Kranti Marg, New Delhi, pp. 102-103.
36. NCDC, *Annual Report,* 2001-02, pp. 16-17.

ANNEXURE-A

REPORT OF THE COMMITTEE ON MODEL COOPERATIVES ACT

Review of the Status of the Cooperative Movement

History of cooperative legislation in India dates back to 1904 when the first Cooperative Societies Act was passed. The approach of the Government in framing the cooperative law was stated by Sir Denzil Ibbets on in the following words- "Certain broad principles must be laid down and certain precautions must be insisted upon; but within those principles and subject to those precautions, the people must in the main be left to work out their own salvation on their own lines, the functions of government being confined to hearty sympathy, assistance and advice."

The Cooperative Credit Societies Act (1904) was restrictive in its scope, as it permitted only primary credit societies and kept non-credit and federal societies out of its purview. The Cooperative Societies Act of 1912 removed many of these shortcomings and served as a model for subsequent Acts passed by various State Governments when 'cooperative societies' became a transferred subject under the constitutional reforms of 1919.

The Rural Credit Survey Committee, 1954 recommended that promotion of cooperatives be accepted as a part of state policy in the development of various economic activities, particularly in those providing support to agriculture. The policy led to state partnership in the share capital of cooperatives and in their management. Committee on Cooperative Law (1955) appointed by the Government of India suggested a number of modifications in the cooperative legislation for giving effect to the concept of the state partnership and accordingly various State Cooperative Societies' Acts were amended which in effect also strengthened the government control on the cooperative institutions.

In 1958, the National Development Council adopted a Cooperative Policy Resolution, which inter-alia, also examined the cooperative legislative framework. The Council had observed: "many of the existing procedures impede the development of cooperation as a popular movement in which small groups and communities can function freely and organize their work and activities along the cooperative lines without excessive official interference and red tap. The restrictive features of existing cooperative legislation should be removed and both the present cooperative laws and model legislation and rules which have been under consideration of the states should be modified in accordance with the approach outlined in this Resolution".

Subsequent expert committees/working groups have influenced the court of cooperative legislation are committee on Cooperative Administration (1963); Mirdha Committee on Cooperation (1965); Working Group on Cooperation of Administrative reforms Commission (1967); and the recommendations of various Committees and cooperative congress convened by the National Cooperative Union of India. The Committee on Cooperative Administration while examining the role of Registrar Cooperative Societies felt that in order to make cooperative movement the peoples' movement in real sense of the term and to foster popular initiative within the cooperative movement, it is necessary that the role of Registrar should be confined to that of a "friend, philosopher and guide" to the cooperative movement and many of the powers which have concentrated in his hands should be transferred to the federal cooperative organizations. The Committee observed, "each sector of the movement should ultimately have its own federal arrangements for supervision". It further added, "the work of supervising non-credit type of societies may be transferred from cooperative departments to the federal cooperative organizations are not strong enough, the Committee recommended that the Government by giving catalytic help to the cooperative movement should promote these federal organizations to which ultimately some of the statutory powers of the Registrar Cooperative Societies should be transferred.

The Committee on Cooperation (1965), popularly known as Mirdha Committee, gave a new orientation to cooperative law. The Committee analysed criteria of genuine cooperative societies and removal of vested interest from them. However, on the pretext of promotion of genuine cooperative movement by removing vested interests, the state governments made cooperative legislation more and more restrictive and stringent pushing cooperative character of the movement in the background.

The Working Group on Cooperative of Administrative Reforms Commission (1967) also propounded similar thinking as given by the Mirdha promotion of cooperation as people's movement full of self-regulation and self-control. In view of this the powers of audit, supervision and control that vest, presently, with the Registrar Cooperative Societies should be gradually passed on the federal bodies of the cooperative institutions. However, the Registrar should continue to exercise checks and balances in order to maintain steady growth of the cooperative movement based on cooperative principles.

The conference of chief ministers and state ministers for cooperation which met at Madras in 1968 considered certain important aspects of management of cooperatives with a view to stem the growth of vested interest in cooperative and to ensure that economic benefits conferred by cooperatives flow in a larger measure to the weaker sections of the community. This conference suggested certain legislative measures to be introduced relating to:

a) Exclusion of moneylenders etc. from becoming members of cooperatives;

b) Reservation of seats on the board of management of cooperatives for weaker sections;

c) Restriction on holding office for more than the prescribed term;

d) Restriction on holding office simultaneously in a number of institutions;

e) Regulation of loans to office-bearers;

f) Regular election by an independent authority.

The recommendations of the Chief Ministers' Conference of 1968 were accepted by the States and legislative changes made. In the process, many state governments amended their Acts to give additional powers to the government as well as government nominees on the board of directors of cooperatives. These related to the power of veto of board decisions, issue of directives to cooperatives by Government/Registrar, appointment of personnel in cooperatives as also approval of the terms and conditions of their service. These provisions have led to progressive erosion of the autonomy of cooperatives, an essential concomitant to their democratic character.

Committee on Cooperative Law (Ardhanareeswaran Committee) in its Report in 1987, have examined various State Cooperative Acts and made the following observations:

- The existing Cooperative Societies Act contain provisions which militate against the democratic character and the autonomy of cooperatives.

- Over the years, the Registrar has acquired undue powers in respect of management decisions of the cooperatives, which should be curtailed.

- The role of the Registrar should be made more positive and he should be looked upon as a development agent.

- The federal cooperative societies should play a more active part in the developmental functions relating to promotion, organization, proper functioning and growth of the affiliated cooperative societies.

The changing complexities of member management, human resource development, financial management have necessitated availability of professional assistance to cooperatives through adequate trained and professional paid staff on appropriate terms working under the general guidance of a democratically elected body.

Review of the Current Situation

The essence of cooperative organization is the principle of democratic management, signifying institutional regulation by the members and their elected representatives in accordance with the bye-laws. It precludes control and interference by any outside agency including Government, except the usual penal action by the competent statutory authority in proven cases of abuse. The cooperative law has to respect this aspect of cooperative organization.

However, trends that have developed during the post-independence period present an altogether different picture. Fast as has been the growth of cooperative activity through increased governmental aid, stronger and tighter has been the control of the Government over the movement through incorporation of restrictive features in cooperative legislation stultifying cooperative leadership, generating members apathy and curbing local initiative at grass-root level.

A brief analysis of the restrictive provisions now in force is presented in succeeding paras.

Compulsory Amendment of Bye-laws by the Registrar

The provision that exists almost in all the States provides unfettered power to the Registrar of Cooperative Societies to direct a society or class of societies to amend their bye-laws. Ideologically speaking, the bye-laws represent self-imposed constitutional framework by the members and nay power to affect amendment therein should rest with the members and their General Body.

The Power of Government to Nominate Directors on the Committee of Management

Almost in all the Cooperative Societies Acts of the Stats, the State Governments have been empowered to nominate on the Board of Management of Cooperative Societies a certain number of Directors. While in some of the states the right of the States the right of the Government is restricted to the nomination of three Directors or 1/3rd of the strength on the Board of Directors whichever is less, some of the States have assumed much larger powers in the appointment of Chairman and Managing Director in Cooperative Societies where the Government have contributed to their share capital. Such provisions are an utter negation of the principle of self-regulation. They prevent the development of democratic leadership, dampen initiative and convert cooperatives into a playground of politics.

Power of Government to Veto Annual/Recind Resolutions

Some Cooperative Societies Acts authorize the Government nominee to refer any decision of the Board of Management to the Government whose decision shall be final provided the Government have subscribed to the share capital or hold interest by way of guarantee or borrowings to the extent 50% of working capital of the society. Similarly, in other States Government nominee is empowered to refer any resolution of the society to the Government, if he feels that the same is prejudicial to the interest of the Government nominees, who often, in the name of safeguarding the interest of the Government. Such provisions provide unlimited power to the government nominees, who often, in the name of safeguarding the interest of the Government, meddle with the democratic functioning of the cooperative institutions.

Power of Registrar/State Government to give Directives

Under the provisions the Registrar of Cooperative Societies or State Governments have been clothed with wide powers of issuing directions to the cooperative societies. Such provision exists in many States of the country. Through such provision the Registrar of Cooperative Societies may usurp the rightful jurisdiction of the elected management of cooperatives to formulate their policies and programmes.

Supersession/Suspension of Committee of Management

These provisions, though incorporated for prosecuting mismanagement for abuse of office, have been misused for "extra-cooperative" consideration and furtherance of political interest. Usually in every cooperative societies act certain safeguards such as issue of show cause notice to the society before superseding its committee of management, consultation with financing institutions; limiting the period of supersession, have been provided. However, in actual practice when consideration other than those intended in the Act came into play, such safeguards are manoveured wrongfully to gain the ulterior end.

The Cooperatives Societies Acts of Punjab, Haryana, Madhya Pradesh, Himachal Pradesh, Orissa have added further rigors to such provisions by empowering the Registrar to suspend the Committee of Management even during the pendency of the action initiated for the supersession of the Managing Committee. This virtually negates all the safeguards that may have been provided in the Act by way of reasonable opportunities to explain before any action is taken.

Automatic Supersession of the Committee of Management of Cooperative Credit Societies

Following the implementation of the recommendations of the Study Team on "Overdues in Cooperative Credit Institutions" a very rigorous provision for automatic supersession of the Board of

Management of the Central Cooperative Banks and Primary Credit Societies has been incorporated in many of the cooperative societies Acts, in case the overdues of cooperatives loans exceed a prescribed percentage. The bad recovery position, many a times, is on account of political acts and directives. The recent loan waiver scheme of the government is one such instance.

Restriction on Term of Office of Office Bearers of Cooperative Societies

Following the implementation of the recommendations of the Conferences of Chief Ministers and Ministers of Cooperation held in 1968, provisions were incorporated to restrict the period and the number of terms for which an individual could continuously hold certain elected offices on the committee of management of a cooperative society. These provisions have been incorporated in almost all the State Cooperative Societies Act.

Restriction on Holding Office in a Number of Cooperatives Simultaneously

Restrictions were imposed in almost all the States following the recommendations of Chief Ministers' Conference held in 1968, which debarred an individual from holding any specified office at the same time in more than the prescribed number of cooperative societies.

Compulsory Amalgamation and Division of Societies by the Registrar

Almost all Cooperative Acts have a provision which empowers the Registrar Cooperative Societies to effect compulsory division and amalgamation of cooperative institutions if it is in the interest of the cooperative movement. The power to effect amalgamation or division, contained in the Cooperative Acts in India, is underemocratic and in practice has been used even without taking the institutions affected into confidence or giving regard to their individual problems and needs.

The Main Thrust of Model Cooperative Act

The Model Cooperative Societies Act has been drafted by the Planning Commission in the background of prevailing situation of the Cooperative Movement in the country; existing nature of Cooperative laws at the centre and in the States governing cooperatives; persistent demands of the cooperative the present and previous governments to change the laws.

The approach of the model law is to give a genuine character to cooperatives, to facilitate building of an integrated cooperative structure so as to evolve a cooperative system, make the federal organizations at various levels more responsive and responsible towards their members, to minimize government control and interference to enable cooperators and cooperatives to develop self-reliance and self-confidence with power of decision making and to eliminate politicization. The draft law, thus, removes the colonical approach and character of existing laws and truly meets the norms of governance of a democratic autonomous enterprise in the country so deeply committed to democratic values.

Special Features of the Model Cooperatives Act

State policy on cooperatives and the principles of cooperation have been stated in the beginning of the Act as a guide to the remaining provisions of the Model Act and to facilitate the government to conform to the basic ideology of cooperation.

Procedure for Registration of a new cooperative is simplified and all artificial restrictions by way of area of operation, economic viability etc. are removed.

The Model Act gives no rule making power to the government. The law itself lays down the broad parameters necessarily to be observed by cooperatives and leaves all other matters relating to constitution, management and business of the society to be conducted in accordance with its bye-laws.

The Model Act gives no power to the Registrar or the Government issue to orders for any of the following in a cooperative:

a) Supersession of the Board of Director;

b) Compulsory amalgamation or division of societies;

c) Compulsory amendment of the bye-laws;

d) Veto/rescind/annual the resolution;

e) Issue directives.

Cooperative Federations/Unions are to assume greater responsibility towards the member cooperatives and in particular to ensure regular conduct of election to the Board of Management and timely conduct of annual audit of accounts.

The Role of the Registrar under the Model Act has been confined to the registration and liquidation of cooperatives, conduct of inquiry and in case of default to conduct election, audit and to convene meeting of general body.

The Model Act prohibits cooperatives from accepting funds from the Government by way of equity.

To ensure the character of cooperative as a member user organization, special obligations have been imposed on members.

Board of Directors have been made accountable for timely conduct of elections, regular convening of meetings of the managing committee and the general body and for participation therein and for the timely conduct of the audit of the books of accounts.

Model Act prohibits officers of the government to work in a cooperative.

The Model Act provides for the Constitution of Cooperative Tribunal for settlement of disputes including appeals on matters relating to constitution, management and business of a cooperative and to take cognizance of any offence under the Act.

Part II

__________________Cooperatives Act, 19__________Contents

Chapter – VI: Management

25. Membership
26. Termination of membership
27. General body
28. Board of directors
29. Powers and functions of the board
30. Term of office
31. Elections
32. Meetings
33. Staff

Chapter – VII: Information

35. Minutes
36. Accounts and records to be maintained
37. Audit
38. Filing of returns
39. Inquiry

Chapter – VIII: Settlement of disputes

40. Settlement of disputes
41. Constitution of cooperative courts

Chapter – IX: Offences and penalties

42. Offences
43. Penalties
44. Authority to take congnizance

Chapter – X: Dissolution

45. Dissolution by members
46. Dissolution by registrar
47. Dissolution by court
48. Duties of liquidator
49. Powers of liquidator

50 Final account

Chapter – XI: Miscellaneous

51. Enabling provision for different cooperatives

Chapter – I

Introduction

1. Preamble

In order to facilitate the voluntary formation and democratic functioning of cooperatives as people's institutions based on self-help and mutual aid and to enable people to promote their economic and social betterment, the legislature of the state of ____________ in the ______________ year of the Republic of India do hereby enact as follows:

2. State Policy on Cooperatives

It shall be the policy of the State to promote cooperatives which are instruments of equity, social justice and economic development in fulfillment of the Directive Principles of the State Policy as enshrined in the Indian Constitution.

3. Cooperative Principles

The following shall constitute the cooperative principles:

(i) Membership of a cooperative shall be voluntary and available without artificial restriction or any social political, racial or religious discrimination, to all persons who can make use of its services are willing to accept the responsibilities of membership.

(ii) Cooperatives are democratic organizations. Their affairs shall be administered by persons elected or appointed in a manner agreed by the members and accountable to them. Members of primary cooperatives shall enjoy equal rights of voting (one member, one vote) and participation in decisions affecting their cooperatives. In other than primary cooperatives, the administration shall be conducted on a democratic basis in a suitable form.

(iii) Share capital shall only receive a strictly limited rate of interest, if any.

(iv) The economic results, arising out of the operations of a cooperative belong to the members of that cooperative and shall be distributed in such a manner as would avoid one member gaining at the expense of others.

This may be done by decision of the members as follows:

a) by provision for development of the business of the cooperatives;

b) by provision of common services; or

c) by distribution among the members in promotion to their transactions with the cooperative.

(v) All cooperatives shall make provision for the education of their members, officers and employees and of the general public, in the principles and techniques of cooperation, both economic and democratic.

(vi) All cooperatives, in order to best serve the interest of their members and their communities, shall actively cooperate in every practical way with other cooperatives at local, national and international levels having as their aim the achievement of unity of action by cooperators throughout the world.

4. Short title, extent and commencement

1) This Act may be called the _______________Cooperatives' Act 19

2) It extends to the whole of the state of _________________

3) It shall come into force on such date as the government may notify in the _________________gazette.

5. Definitions

In this Act, unless the context otherwise requires

a. "area of operation" means the area from which the membership is drawn;

b. "board of directors" means the governing body of a society by whatever name called;

c. "byelaws" means the registered byelaws for the time being in force;

d. "chief executive" means an individual who, subject to the superintendence, control and direction of the board of directors, has been entrusted by the board, with the management of the affairs of the cooperative;

e. "cooperative" means an organization registered or deemed to be registered under this Act;

f. "cooperative basis" means in consonance with the cooperative principles enumerated in this Act;

g. "federal cooperative" means a cooperative whose membership is available only to cooperatives;

h. "general body" in relation to a primary cooperative means all the members of that cooperative and in relation to a federation, means all the delegates of the member cooperatives;

i. "general meeting" means a meeting of the general body of a cooperatives;

j. "member" means a person admitted as such to a cooperative;

k. "officer" means a person elected or appointed by a cooperative to any office of such cooperative;

l. "patronage refund" means annual refund to members in proportion to their transactions with the cooperative during the year;

m. "registrar" means the registrar of cooperatives appointed under section 16 and includes any other person on whom all or any of the powers of the registrar under this Act are conferred;

n. "state" means the state of ____________________.

o. "primary cooperative" means a cooperative whose membership is available only to individuals.

Chapter – II

Incorporation

6. Organization may be registered

1) Only such an organization may be registered as a cooperative under this Act which provide in its byelaws for the social and economic betterment of its members through self help and mutual aid in accordance with the cooperative principles.

2) A cooperative shall be registered with limited liability.

7. Application for registration

1) An application for registration shall be submitted to the registrar by hand or by registered post.

2) Every such application shall be accompanied by

   a. two copies of the proposed byelaws of the cooperative as adopted by the promoting members;

   b. a list of names of members with their addresses, occupation and equity participation;

   c. the list of members of the first board elected by the promoting members;

   d. a true copy of the minutes of the meeting at which the byelaws were adopted, duly signed by the chairperson.

3) Every such application shall be signed by at least 10 individuals from different families, in the case of a proposed primary

cooperative and by authorized representatives of atleast 2 primary cooperatives, in the case of a proposed federal cooperative.

4) The registrar shall register the cooperative and also its byelaws and communicate by registered post the certificate of registration and a copy of the registered bylaws, within sixty days from the date of submission of application, to the chairperson.

5) The registrar, if the conditions laid down in sub-section(3) are not fulfilled, shall communicate by registered post the order of refusal together with the reason therefore, within sixty days from the date of submission of application, to such of the applicants as specified in the application.

6) In case no refusal is communicated within 60 days, the cooperative shall be deemed to be registered.

7) Where a cooperative is registered, the registrar shall issue a certificate of registration signed and sealed by him which shall be conclusive evidence that the cooperative mentioned therein, is a cooperative duly registered under this Act.

8) Where an order of refusal is received by the applicants under sub-clause(5), they may appeal against this order to the cooperative tribunal. The decision of the tribunal shall be final in this regard.

8. Cooperative to be a body corporate

1) The registration of a cooperative shall render it a body corporate by the name under which it is registered having perpetual succession and a common seal. The cooperative shall be entitled to acquire, hold and dispose of property, to enter into contracts on its behalf, to institute and defend suits and other legal proceedings and to do all other things necessary to achieve its objectives.

2) All transactions entered into a good faith prior to registration, in furtherance of the purposes of the cooperative, shall be deemed to be transactions of the cooperative after registration.

9. Display of name

1) Every cooperative shall display its name and the address of its registered office and the words 'Registered under ______________Cooperatives' Act 19 'in legible characters in a conspicuous position.

a. at every office or place at which it carries on business;

b. in all notices and other official publications;

c. on all its contracts, business letters, orders for goods, invoices, statements of account, receipts and letters of credit; and

d. on all bills of exchange, promissory notes, endorsements, cheques and orders for money it signs or that are signed on its behalf.

2) The name of every cooperative shall contain the words 'cooperative' and 'limited' or their equivalent in the official language of the state.

10. Appointment of registrar

1) The state government may appoint a registrar such other offices as its thinks necessary for the registration of cooperatives under this Act and for such other functions as specified under this Act.

2) Only such persons may be appointed as registrar as have:

a) served as a senior officer of the government for atleast 3 years in the cooperative department; or

b) served as chief executive for atleast 3 years in any cooperative; or

c) held a senior officer or faculty position for atleast 3 years in any cooperative promotional body or academic institution dealing with cooperation.

3) The team of office of a registrar shall be at least three years.

Chapter – III

Bye-Laws

11.Bye-laws

1) Except on such specific matters which the Act has provided for and which the byelaws may further regulate on but not contravene, the functioning of every cooperative shall be regulated by its byelaws.

2) The byelaws of a cooperative may provide for the following matters:

a. the name, address and area of operation of the cooperative

b. the objective of the cooperative explicitly stated as a common central need of the members;

c. the cooperative principles as stated in this Act, according to which the cooperative shall conduct its affairs;

d. the services to be provided to its members

e. eligibility for obtaining membership

f. procedure for obtaining membership

g. conditions for continuing as member

h. the time limit before which a potential member must seek and obtain membership in order to continue to use the services of the cooperatives

i. procedure for withdrawal/transfer of membership

j. procedure for termination and cessation of membership

k. rights of members

l. fixation of minimum performance required annually of each member vis-à-vis use of services, financial commitment and participation in meetings, in order to be eligible to exercise the rights of membership including the right of vote.

m. the consequences of default in payment of any sum due by a member;

n. the nature and amount of capital, if any, of the cooperative;

o. the maximum capital to which a single member can subscribe;

p. the nature and extent of the liability of the members for the debts contracted by the cooperative;

q. the sources and types of funds to be raised by the cooperative;

r. the purposes for which the funds may be applied;

s. the extent and conditions under which deposits, loans, debentures and other funds may be mobilized;

t. the conditions and purposes for which state aid and aid from other financial institutions may be sought and obtained;

u. the manner of disposal of surplus;

v. the constitution of various funds, reserves and their purpose;

w. the manner of convening general and other special meetings and quorum thereof;

x. the frequency of general meetings;

y. the role of the general body and subjects which shall be dealt with by the general body;

z. the manner of making or amending byelaws;

aa. the procedure for conducting elections

bb. the procedure for conducting election in case the cooperative fails to do so;

cc. the size and constitution of the board of directors

dd. eligibility for becoming director;

ee. conditions for retaining directorship;

ff. the terms of office of the directors and for filling of vacancies;

gg. the procedure for removal of directors and for filling of vacancies;

hh. the manner of convening board meetings and quorum

ii. the frequency of board meetings;

jj. powers and functions of the board;

kk. powers and functions of office bearers including chairperson;

ll. powers and functions of the chief executive;

mm. penalties for acting against the interests of members and for non-fulfilment of duties by members, directors and staff;

nn. the appointment and role of auditors and procedure for conduct of audit where the cooperative fail to make necessary arrangements and time limit for audit compliance;

oo. the authorization of an officer or officers to sign documents and to institute and defend suits and other legal proceedings on behalf of the cooperative;

pp the terms on which a cooperative may deal with non-members;

qq. the terms on which a cooperative may associate with other cooperatives;

rr. the terms on which a cooperative may deal with organizations other than cooperatives;

ss. the rights, if any, which the cooperative may confer on any cooperative or other federations and the circumstances under which these rights may be exercised by the federation/s;

tt. the manner of disposal of funds if under liquidation;

uu. the accounting year for the cooperatives;

vv. transfer of shares and interest in the name of a nominee in case of death of a member;

ww. the manner of dissolution of the cooperative;

xx. restriction, if any, on service to non-members;

yy. organize self-help groups of people living in its area and to conduct education and training programmes.

12. Amendment of bye-laws

1) A cooperative may amend any of its byelaws by a resolution passed at a general meeting by a majority of the total membership with right of vote or of two thirds of members present and voting whichever is less;

Provided no such resolution shall be passed by the general body unless at least twenty clear days of written notice of the resolution and of the general meeting has been given alongwith a copy of the proposed amendment to each member of the cooperative.

2) An application for the registration of the amendment shall be forwarded by registered post to the registrar within a period of thirty days from the date of the resolution.

3) Every application forwarded to the registrar shall be signed by the chairperson and two members of the committee and shall be accompanied by the following particulars.

   a. a copy of the resolution adopting the amendment;

   b. the date of the general meeting at which the amendment was approved;

   c. the date of the notice issued for the general meeting;

   d. the total number of members on the rolls of the cooperative having the right of vote on the date of such general meeting;

   e. the number of members having the right of vote present at such general meeting; and

   f. the number of members who voted for the resolution.

4) The registrar, if the proposed amendment is in consonance with the provisions of the Act, shall register the amendment within a period of sixty days from the date of receipt of the application.

5) The registrar shall forward to the cooperative within a period of 15 days after registration, a copy of the registered amendment together with a certificate signed and sealed by him, and such certificate shall be conclusive proof that the amendment has been duly registered.

6) The registrar, if the proposed amendment is not in consonance with the provisions of the Act, shall communicate by registered

post the order of refusal together with the reasons therefore to the cooperative within the period specified in sub-section(4);

Provided that no order refusing to register the amendment shall be passed except after giving the cooperative an opportunity of making its representation.

7) Where no order of refusal is communicated under sub-section (6) within the period specified in that sub-section, it shall be deemed that the registrar has registered the amendment on the last date of the period specified in that sub-section.

13. Change of liability, transfer of assets and liabilities, division, amalgamation of a cooperative

1) A cooperative may, be a resolution of its general body, decide to change the extent of its limited liability;

2) A cooperative may, by a resolution of its general body, decide to transfer its assets and liabilities, in whole or in part, to any other cooperative which agrees to such transfer by a resolution of its general body;

3) A cooperative may, by a resolution of its general body, divide itself into two or more cooperatives;

4) Any two or more cooperatives may, by a resolution of their respective general bodies, decide to amalgamate themselves and form a new cooperative;

5) Every resolution of a cooperative under this section shall be passed at its general meeting by a majority of total members with right of vote or two thirds of members present and voting whichever is less and such resolution shall contain all particulars of the liability, transfer, division, amalgamation as the case may be.

6) Where a cooperative has passed a resolution under this section, it shall give notice thereof together with a copy of the resolution

to all its members, federal cooperatives to which it is affiliated and creditors who may give their consent. Otherwise, notwithstanding any byelaw or contract to the contrary, any member, federal cooperative or creditor shall, during a period of one month from the date of service of the notice have the option of withdrawing their shares, deposits, loans, or services as the case may be.

7) Any member, federal cooperative or creditor who or which does not exercise within the specified period the right under sub-section(6) shall be deemed to have assented to the resolution.

8) A resolution passed by a cooperative under this section shall not take effect until:

a(i) all the members, federal cooperatives and creditors have assented or are deemed to have assented to the resolution under sub-section (6) or sub-section(7) or

(ii) all claims of the members, federal cooperatives and creditors who have exercised the option referred to under sub-section(7) with the period specified therein have been met in full or otherwise satisfied; and

b(i) in the case of change of liability, amendment of the byelaws of the cooperative concerned is registered or deemed to have been registered; or

(ii) in the case of division or amalgamation, the certificate or registration of the cooperative, or the cooperatives, as the case may be, is issued or deemed to have been issued.

9) When a resolution passed by a cooperative under sub-section(2) takes effect the resolution shall be a sufficient conveyance to vest the assets and liabilities in the transferee without any further assurance.

10) The registration of a cooperative shall stand cancelled and the cooperative shall be deemed to have been dissolved and shall cease to exist as a corporate body:

   a. when the whole of the assets and liabilities of such cooperative are transferred to another cooperative; or

   b. when such cooperative divides itself into two or more cooperatives.

11) Where two or more cooperatives are amalgamated into a new cooperative, the registration of the cooperatives so amalgamated shall stand cancelled and they shall be deemed to have been dissolved and shall cease to exist as corporate bodies.

14. Promotion of subsidiary organization

1) Any cooperative may, by a resolution passed at general meeting by a majority of members present and voting, promote one more subsidiary organizations for the furtherance of its stated objectives, and such organization or organizations may be registered under any law for the time being in force, as agreed to by the general body.

2) The annual reports and accounts of any such subsidiary organization shall be placed before the general meeting of the promoting cooperative each year.

3) Any subsidiary organization created under sub-section(1) shall exist only as long as general body of the cooperative deems its existence necessary.

15. Partnership of cooperatives

Any two or more cooperatives may, by resolutions passed at general meetings by a majority of members present and voting in each such cooperative, enter into a contract of partnership for carrying out any specific business permissible under the byelaws on such terms and conditions as may be mutually agreed upon.

Where such partnership requires the creation of a new organization, the participating cooperatives shall be its members.

Chapter – IV

Federations

16. Cooperative Federations/Unions

1) Federal cooperative organizations/cooperative unions consisting of primary and/or secondary cooperatives as members may be established and shall be eligible for registration under this Act.

2) For serving their constituent and in accordance with their byelaws, federal cooperatives/unions may perform the following functions:

   a. safeguard the observance of the cooperative principles;

   b. promote and organize cooperatives and for this purpose, frame model byelaws and guidelines for framing various regulations and policies for consideration by cooperatives;

   c. provide cooperative training, education and information, and propagate cooperative principles;

   d. undertake research and evaluation and assist in preparation of perspective development plans of members cooperatives;

   e. promote harmonious relations between member cooperatives;

   f. help member cooperatives in the settlement of disputes among themselves and between a cooperative and its members;

g. represent the interests of member cooperatives and lobby for policies and legislation favourable to cooperatives;

h. undertake business services on behalf of its members;

i. provide cooperative and management development services to member cooperatives including participation in board meetings where invited;

j. to prepare a panel of auditors and ensure timely conduct of annual audit in member cooperatives;

k. ensure timely conduct of elections in member cooperatives;

l. assist member cooperatives in regular conduct of general meetings;

m. evolve code of conduct for observance by member cooperatives;

n. evolve viability norms for member cooperatives;

o. provide legal aid and advice;

p. assist member cooperatives in organizing self-help groups of people living in its area;

q. provide any other services, at the behest of member cooperatives.

3. a. A federal cooperative may request the board of directors of a member cooperative to convene a general body meeting of its members and shall request the board to do so where at least 10% of the members of the member cooperative have requested the federation to do so.

b. The board of directors of the member cooperative shall convene such a meeting within 30 days of receipt of the requisition. The requisition shall contain the items to be included in the agenda and these shall be dealt with at the general meeting.

c. Where a member cooperative fails to convene a general meeting within 30 days of receipt of a requisition to do so by a federal cooperative, the board of directors of the federal cooperative may themselves call such meeting for dealing with such items as included in the requisition.

4) a. General body of a federal cooperative shall consist of the delegates from the member cooperatives;

b. The chairperson of a cooperative shall ordinarily be the delegate to the next tier of cooperative provided, however, that if the chairperson is unable to so represent for any reason, he may nominate the chief executive or any other member of the board to be the delegate.

c. The delegate shall continue to represent his/her cooperative in the federal cooperative as long as he/she remains in office in the member cooperative.

5) A cooperative union may

i) create and maintain the cooperative education fund;

ii) represent the interests and welfare of all types of cooperatives at district and state level;

iii) promote new forms of cooperative enterprise;

iv) undertake experimental projects towards the application of cooperative ideology;

v) liaise on behalf of and amongst cooperatives;

vi) serve as a data bank on cooperation.

Chapter – V

Management of Funds

17. Mobilization of funds

A cooperative may mobilize equity capital, deposits, debentures, loans and other contributions from its members to such extent and under such conditions as may be specified in the byelaws.

18. Restriction on borrowings

1) A cooperative may mobilize debentures, deposits, raise loans and receive grants from external sources to such extent and under such conditions as may be specified in the byelaws. Deposits and loans raised from external sources, however, shall at no time exceed ten times the sum of member funds and organizational reserves less accumulated deficit if any.

2) A cooperative may accept funds from the government or other financing institution for the fulfillment of its objectives on such terms and conditions as are mutually contracted upon and such conditions may include the right of the government or other financier to nominate one expert on the board of directors.

19. Restriction on holding of equity

1) No member in a primary cooperative shall, at any time, hold more than one tenth of the paid up equity capital.

2) No cooperative shall accept funds from the government by way of equity.

20. Disposal of surplus

1) In any year a cooperative shall, out of the surplus arising from transactions with members in that year, make deferred payment to members as patronage rebate, an amount more than 20%

but less than 50% of such surplus and make interest payment on share capital at a rate not exceeding the prevailing rate of interest available to depositors in cooperative bank.

2) The balance surplus accruing from members and the entire surplus accruing from transactions with others, shall be utilized in the following manner.

a. Not less than 255 shall be transferred to a statutory reserve fund;

b. Not less than 20% shall be transferred to a reserve for meeting unforeseen losses;

c. Where the cooperative is a member of the cooperative union, upto 3% may be transferred to a cooperative education fund with the cooperative union;

d. Bonus shall be paid to employees in accordance with the decision of the general body;

e. Not less than 20% shall be transferred to an equity redemption fund by such cooperatives as already have government equity participation;

f. Not less than 5% may be transferred towards a common good fund whose purpose is approved by the general body;

g. Not more than 5% may be paid as contribution for any purpose connected with the development of the cooperative movement;

h. The balance shall be transferred to such other funds and reserves as created by the general body;

i. Surplus accruing as a result of servicing persons other than members shall not be divisible amongst members and may be utilized towards equity participation of potential members.

21. Liability of deficit

Where a cooperative has an operational deficit in any given year the board of directors shall place before the general body the amount of and reasons for the deficit.

22. Reserve and other funds

1) A cooperative may create statutory and non statutory reserves and other funds for the promotion of the objects of the cooperative.

2) Reserves and other funds shall be used for the purpose for which they were created when necessary but otherwise may be used in the business of the cooperative.

23. Investment of funds outside the business

Such of its funds as are not needed for use by a cooperative may be invested or deposited outside its business:

a. in any federal cooperative of which it is a member;

b. in a local cooperative or nationalized bank;

c. in the equities of any other cooperative;

d. in any of the securities specified in section 20 of the Indian Trust Act, 1882;

e. in the local postal savings bank.

24. Restriction on contribution

No cooperative shall make a contribution either in money or in kind, either directly or indirectly to an organization that has as an object the furtherance of the interests of a political party or of any religious faith.

Chapter VI

Management

25. Membership

1) Any person, who needs the services of the cooperative, accepts the responsibilities of membership and fulfils such other conditions as may be specified in the byelaws of the cooperative, and is competent to contract may be admitted as a member.

2) Membership shall be available as provided for in the cooperative principles without any discrimination on grounds of sex.

3) Every cooperative shall organize, a cooperative educational course for all persons seeking membership and for existing members and shall provide funds each year for cooperative education and training of its members, staff and directors and to organize into self-help groups people living in its area to promote collective action for their economic development.

4) Admission of members may be made only by an elected board of directors or by the general body where such a board does not exist.

5) In addition to such disqualifications as may be contained in the byelaws of a cooperative, the following restrictions shall apply for obtaining and retaining membership in a cooperative:

a. ineligibility of a person to obtain or retain membership where the person's business in conflict or competition with such business of the cooperative as specified in the byelaws;

b. ineligibility of the person to retain membership where the person has not used for 2 consecutive years, the services of the cooperative to the minimum level specified in the byelaws and such non-performance has not been condoned by the general body.

c. ineligibility of the person to retain membership where the person has not attended 3 consecutive general meetings of the cooperative and such absence has not received the consent of the general body;

d. ineligibility of a person to retain membership where the person is in default regarding any payment to be made to the cooperative, exceeding an amount and for a period specified in the byelaws.

No cooperative shall, without sufficient cause, refuse admission to any person duly qualified for membership under the byelaws. Where admission is so refused, the decision with the reasons shall be communicated by registered post to such person within fifteen days of the date of decision, or within thirty days from the date of application for membership, whichever is earlier;

Provided that if no such decision is communicated within thirty days of applying for membership, then the person shall be deemed to have been admitted as a member of the cooperative on the thirty first day.

Where a person has been refused membership by the board of directors, an appeal shall lie to the general body against the decision of the board. Any applicant aggrieved by the decision of the general body may apply to the cooperative tribunal for review of the decision.

26. Termination of membership

1) The board of directors may, by a resolution passed by a majority of the total number of members of the board having the right to vote and not less than two third of the members present and voting, terminate the membership of a person in the cooperative for acts/omissions which are detrimental to

the proper working of the cooperative, provided that the membership shall not be so terminated without giving the person a reasonable opportunity of making representation in this regard.

2) Where membership of a person has been terminated by the board of directors an appeal shall lie to the general body and the decision of the general body shall be final.

3) No person whose membership has been terminated shall be eligible for re-admission as a member of the cooperative for a period of one year from the date of such termination.

27. Restriction on services to non-members

A cooperative's services shall ordinarily be available only to members unless otherwise provided in the byelaws.

28. General body

1) Subject to the provisions of this Act and the byelaws, the ultimate authority of a cooperative shall vest in its general body.

2) Where a cooperative so desires, its byelaws may provide for a representative general body drawn from the members, to be constituted in such a manner and with such functions as specified in the byelaws; any reference in this Act to the general body shall apply to the representative general body where this exists.

3) Subject to the other provisions of this Act, and of the byelaws the following matters shall be dealt with by the general body:

a. election of directors of the board;

b. removal of directors of the board and filling up of vacancies;

c. consideration of the annual report presented by the board;

d. appointment and removal of statutory auditors and internal auditors;

e. consideration of the auditor's report and audited statement of accounts;

f. consideration of audit compliance report;

g. report on action taken on inquiry report under section 39, if any;

h. disposal of net surplus;

i. review of operational deficit, if any;

j. approval of the long term perspective plan and the annual operational plan;

k. approval of the annual budget;

l. creation of specific reserves and other funds;

m. review of actual utilization of reserve and other funds;

n. report on membership of the cooperative in other cooperatives;

o. partnership with other cooperatives;

p. review of annual report and accounts of any subsidiary organization;

q. appeal of a person whose application for membership has been rejected or whose membership has been terminated by the board of directors;

r. list of employees recruited who are relatives of directors or of the chief executive;

s. amendment of byelaws;

t. formulation of code of conduct for the directors and officers;

u. note of admission and termination of members;

v. dissolution of the cooperative;

w. such other functions specified in the byelaws;

29. Board of directors

1) The general body of a cooperative shall constitute a board of directors in accordance with the byelaws.

2) The size of the board shall be in accordance with the byelaws. Chief Executive shall be an ex-officio member of the board.

3) In addition to such criteria as may be specified in the byelaws, a person shall be ineligible for being chosen as a director, if he/she

a. has at any time lost the right to vote as a member specified in the byelaws;

b. loses the right to continue as member as specified in section 25(5) and the byelaws;

c. incurs any other disqualification specified in the byelaws.

4) In addition to such criteria as may be specified in the byelaws, a person shall cease to be a director if he/she incurs any of the disqualifications specified in sub-section(3) and/or

a. absents himself/herself from three consecutive board meetings;

b. absents himself/herself from any general body meeting and such absence does not receive consent from the general body;

c. is penalized under this Act.

5) In addition to such criteria as may be specified in the byelaws, all the directors of the board shall incur disqualification for a period of three years for being chosen as directors and shall be ineligible to continue as directors of any cooperative, if during their term as directors of a cooperative.

   a. they did not conduct elections within the time specified in byelaws and before the expiry of their term;

   b. they did not conduct their annual general body meeting within 4 months of closure of the cooperative's accounting year or a requisitioned meeting of the general body.

   c. they did not place the audited accounts along with the reports of the auditors before the general body

   6. With the exception of the first 3 years after the registration of a cooperative, in order to be eligible for being chosen as a director of the board, a member:

   a. shall have been a voting member of the cooperative for atleast 2 years immediately preceding the year of election;

   b. shall have attended the two general body meetings of the cooperative immediately preceding the elections.

30. Powers and functions of the board of directors

The board shall, in accordance with the byelaws, be the authority to

a. admit and terminate membership;

b. elect the chairperson and other office bearers;

c. remove from office the chairperson and other office bearers;

d. appoint and remove the chief executive;

e. fix staff strength;

f. frame policies concerning:

i) organization and provision of services to members;

ii) qualifications, recruitment, service conditions and other staff related matters;

iii) mode of custody and investment of funds;

iv) manner of keeping accounts;

v) mobilization, utilization and investment of various funds;

vi) monitoring and management information systems including statutory returns to be filed;

vii) such other subjects and matters necessary for the effective performance of the cooperative;

g. place the annual report, annual financial statements, plan and budget for the approval of the general body;

h. consider audit and compliance reports and place these before the general body;

i. review membership in other cooperatives;

j. undertake such other functions as delegated by the general body.

2) The chairperson shall be elected by the board of directors from among the elected members and shall, in accordance with the byelaws:

a. preside at meetings of the board and the general body;

b. have a second vote in the event of equality of votes on any matter being decided upon by the board except in matter of elections;

c. exercise such other powers as delegated by the board specified in the policies framed or resolutions adopted by the board;

31. Term of office

The term of office of the directors of the board or, where the byelaws provide for retirement of directors by rotation, the term of office of the individual directors shall be for such period as specified in the bylaws but not exceed three years from the date of assumption of office;

Provided, however, that the term of office can be terminated by the general body at its meeting by a majority of members with right of vote or two third of members present and voting.

Provided further that the first board shall not exceed 12 months from the date of registration of the cooperative.

32. Elections

1) The conduct of elections to the board of directors of a cooperative shall be the responsibility of the incumbent board.

2) Elections shall be conducted in the manner specified in the byelaws before the term of office of the outgoing directors comes to an end.

3) Where a board does not take necessary steps to conduct elections before the expiry of the term of the directors, or, where there are no directors remaining on the board, a minimum of 55 of total members of the cooperative may jointly convene a general meeting of the members, for the purpose of appointing an ad-hoc board of directors for the specific purpose of conducting elections.

4) The term of the ad hoc board so appointed shall not exceed three months.

5) The election of the directors shall take place at the general body meeting.

6) The directors shall hold office for the period for which they were elected and the newly elected directors shall assume office at the end of this period.

7) The directors shall, if the byelaws so permit, be eligible for re-election.

8) It shall be the duty of the federal cooperative to inform the registrar if any member cooperative fails to conduct elections in accordance with the byelaws.

9) where the number of nominees exceeds the number of directors to be elected, the election of directors shall be by secret ballot.

10) Where there is a vacancy on the board of directors and where there is a quorum of directors, the remaining directors may exercise all the powers of the board or may fill the vacancy for the remainder of its term from eligible persons, through cooption, if the period remaining is over 6 months.

11) Where there is a vacancy on the board and where there is not a quorum of directors, the remaining directors shall call a general meeting for the purpose of electing members to fill any vacancies for the remaining period.

12) Where a cooperative fails to conduct elections to the board of directors when due, and the federal cooperative/union has not initiated the election process, the registrar shall cause the election to be conducted on the expiry of 90 days from the date of the election falling due. The cost of conducting such elections shall be borne by the cooperative.

33. Meetings

1) The byelaws of a cooperative shall specify the frequency of and manner in which board and general body meetings shall be held, such however, that not less than 4 board meetings

and 1 general body meeting shall be required to be held in a year.

2) The board shall convene a special general meeting within 30 days of receipt of a requisition to this effect from at least one/tenth of members of the cooperative or as provided in the byelaws and any such requisition shall contain the proposed agenda and the reasons why the meeting is felt necessary.

3) Where a cooperative fails to convene the annual general meeting within due time and the concerned federation has also failed to convene the meeting, the registrar shall on the expiry of 90 days convene the annual general meeting.

34. Staff

1) All staff of the cooperative including the chief executive shall be recruited, appointed, removed and guided in accordance with such personnel policies and service conditions as framed by the board and approved by the general body.

2) The chief executive shall perform such functions as specified in the bye-laws and policies and shall:

a. have general control over the day to day operations of the cooperative;

b. be the person to sue or be sued on behalf of the cooperative;

c. on behalf of the cooperative, have powers to endorse, sign, negotiate cheqeus and other negotiable instruments and operate the bank accounts of the cooperative with such other person as the board may desire;

d. be responsible for staff recruitment discipline, performance and development;

e. on behalf of the cooperative, be the person to enter into agreements or contracts;

f. arrange to maintain proper records and accounts of the cooperative;

g. present the draft annual report and financial statement for the approval of the board, within 30 days of closure of the financial year;

h. convene in consultation with the chairperson, the board and general body meetings in accordance with the bye-laws and record the proceedings thereof;

i. assist the board in the formulation of policies and plans;

j. be accountable to the board;

k. furnish to the board information necessary for monitoring the performance of the cooperative;

l. perform any other function as specified in the byelaws or as decided by a resolution of the board and general body.

3) An officer of the government shall not either during the course of his/her service with the government or for a period of three years thereafter, serve in any capacity with any cooperative.

Chapter VI

Information

35. Minutes of proceedings of general meetings and of board and other meetings

1) Every cooperative shall record in the minutes book, minutes of all proceedings of every general meeting and of every meeting of its board of directors;

2) Such minutes shall be circulated to all persons invited for the meeting within 30 days of the conclusion of the meeting;

3) The minutes so recorded shall be signed by the person who chaired the said meeting or by a director duly authorized by the board who attended the meeting.

36. Accounts and records to be maintained

1) Every cooperative shall keep at its registered office, the following accounts and records:

a. a copy of the state cooperatives Act with amendments made from time to time;

b. the minutes book;

c. registration certificate and a copy of registered byelaws and of the amendments registered from time to time with date of amendment;

d. a copy of the authenticated byelaws of the federal cooperatives of which it is a member and of each of its member cooperatives;

e. account of all sums of money received and expended by the cooperative and their respective purposes;

f. account of all purchases and sales of goods by the cooperative;

g. account of the assets and liabilities of the cooperative;

h. a register showing to total membership and the member-wise use of various services;

i. a list of members with voting rights for the current year updated within 30 days of closure of the financial year;

j. copies of the board policies;

k. annual report and audit report.

Provided that where a cooperative has branch offices, accounts and records related to the branch, shall be available at the registered office for any period, within 25 days of the end of that period.

2) Copies of the Act, byelaws, minutes book, voters' list and such accounts as relate to a member, shall be made available to any member during business hours at a fee to be decided by the cooperative.

3) The books of accounts of every cooperative together with supporting records and vouchers, shall be preserved for such period as may be provided in the byelaws subject to any other laws for the time being in force.

37. Audit

1) A cooperative shall get its accounts audited by an auditor selected from the panel prepared by the federal cooperative;

2) The auditor's report, in addition to the report on the accounts of the cooperative shall also contain a report on the attendance at meetings by directors, loans and advances sanctioned to or the business done with the cooperative by the directors, expenses reimbursed to directors, expenditure on education and training for members, staff, directors and others.

3) It shall be the duty of the board of directors to ensure that annual financial statements and prepared and presented for audit within 45 days of closure of the financial year.

4) The general body shall appoint an auditor for auditing the accounts of the cooperative; provide, however, that it may delegate this function to a federal cooperative.

5) The remuneration of an auditor may be fixed by the board of directors and placed before the general body at its next meeting, for information;

6) The general body may at a special meeting remove an auditor form office by a resolution passed by a majority of the members present and voting,

7) The auditor shall be given notice of every general meeting and will be entitled to attend the meeting;

8) Upon the demand of the auditor of a cooperative, the present or former officers, committee members, members or employees of the cooperative shall furnish such

   a. information and explanation; and

   b. access to records, documents, books, accounts and vouchers of the cooperative as are, in the opinion of the examination and report.

9) Where a cooperative fails to get its annual accounts audited when due, it shall be the responsibility of the cooperative union/federation to get the accounts of the cooperative audited within period of 90 days from the date when the audit was due. The cost of conducting such audit shall be borne by the cooperative.

If the cooperative union/federation is unable to get the audit of the cooperative conducted for any reason, the registrar shall get the accounts of the cooperative audited.

38. Filing of returns

Every year, within 5 months of the closure of the financial year, every cooperative shall file the following information with the registrar of cooperatives:

a. annual report of activities;

b. audited statements of accounts;

c. plan for surplus disposal as approved by the general body;

d. list of names of directors and their terms of office;

e. list of amendments to the byelaws of the cooperative;

f. declaration regarding date of holding of general body meeting and conduct of elections where due.

39. Inquiry

1) The registrar may, on the application of a cooperative to which the cooperative concerned is affiliated, or of a creditor to whom the cooperative is indebted, or of not less than one-third of the members of the committee, or of not less than one-tenth of the total number of members of the cooperative hold an inquiry or cause an inquiry to be made into the specific matters raised in the application relating to the constitution, working and financial condition of the cooperative;

2) the registrar shall order an inquiry only after the receipt of a fee, from the applicant or applicants, deemed sufficient to meet the costs of the inquiry to be conducted;

3) The inquiry shall be completed within a period of four months from the date of ordering the inquiry;

4) The registrar shall, within a period of one month from the date of completion of inquiry, communicate the report of the inquiry:

   a. to the cooperative concerned;

   b. to the applicants and the person designated by the applicants to receive such a report;

   c. to any member of a cooperative, to any federation of which the cooperative is a member, to any creditor on payment of fee specified by the registrar.

Chapter – VIII

Settlement of Disputes

40. Settlement of disputes

If any dispute touching the constitution, management or business of a cooperative arises:

a. among members, past members and persons claiming through members and deceased member; or

b. between a member, past member or a person claiming through a member, past member or deceased member and the cooperative, its board or any officer, agent or employee of the cooperative, or liquidator, past or present, or

c. between the cooperative or its board and any past board, any officer, agent or employee, or any past officer, past agent of past employee or the nominee, heirs or legal representatives of any deceased officer, or deceased employee of the cooperative; or

d. between the cooperative and any other cooperative or between a cooperative and liquidator of another cooperative or between the liquidator of one cooperative and the liquidator of another such disputes shall be referred to the cooperative tribunal which will function as a court of law.

41. Constitution of cooperative tribunals

The state government may, by notification in the official gazette, constitute cooperative tribunals for the adjudication of disputes including appeals under this Act, provided that the tribunal shall be presided by a judicial officer not below the rank of a district judge.

Chapter IX

Offences and Penalties

42. Offences

The following shall constitute offences under this Act:

a. violation of the provisions of the Act and byelaws;

b. failure to hand over the records of the cooperative to the person authorized to have the custody of the records;

c. indulging in fraudulent activities concerning the constitution, management and business of the cooperative;

d. misuse of the funds and property of the cooperative;

e. indulging in the conduct of elections to the managing committee in "corrupt practices" as defined under section 123 of the Representation of People Act, 1951.

43. Penalties

Any person who commits any of the offences specified in Sec. 42 of the Act shall be liable for a fine of Rs. 2,000/- for each of the offences committed, without prejudice to the civil or criminal liability that may arise on such person under any other laws for the time being in force.

44. Authority to take cognizance

The cooperative tribunal shall be the authority to take cognizance of the offences committed under this Act.

Chapter – X

Dissolution

45. Dissolution by members

1) In this section:

a. 'interest" means the interest of a member in a cooperative and includes shares, member loans, deposits and obligations of any kind that:

(i) arise by virtue of the byelaws of the cooperative; and

(ii) are owed by the cooperative to the member.

b. 'unallocated surplus" includes any net proceeds from the scale of asset on dissolution of the cooperative after the liabilities of the cooperative and the claims of creditors, members and others have been satisfied.

2) The general body of a cooperative may authorize the dissolution of the cooperative.

3) The board shall cause a notice for a general meeting to be sent to each member for the purpose of authorizing dissolution.

4) A notice to attend such general meeting shall also be sent to the registrar of cooperative to any federation/s to which the cooperative is affiliated, to any cooperative/s with which a partnership contract has been entered into, to auditors and to any subsidiary organization of the cooperative to attend the meeting.

5) Representatives under sub-section (4) shall have the right to make a presentation to the general body.

6) For the purpose of sub-section(2), dissolution is authorized when the members approve the dissolution by a special resolution of two third of members present and voting.

7) Within 15 days of such authorization for dissolution, the cooperative shall send to the registrar of cooperative a copy of the authorization to dissolve a cooperative, by registered post.

8) The authorization approved in pursuance of sub-section(6) is required to set out:

   a. the assets and liabilities of the cooperative;

   b. the claims of any creditors;

   c. the number of members; and

   d. the nature and extent of the members' interest in the cooperative.

9) When the registrar approves a special resolution passed in pursuance of sub section(6), he shall cause a notice of the special resolution to be published once a week for two weeks in the gazette and in a newspaper having general circulation in the district where the registered office of the cooperative is located.

10) The registrar may require from a cooperative, liquidator or trustee appointed by a cooperative or any other person who is required to furnish information, an annual or other return showing:

   a. the progress of dissolution;

   b. the distribution of any undistributed surplus or reserve;

   c. the progress of the administration of a trust established in accordance with this section; and

   d. any other information that he/she may require..

46. Dissolution by Registrar

1) Where the registrar has reasonable cause to believe that a cooperative:

   a. has not commenced business within two years after the date shown on its certificate of registration; or

b. has not carried on business for two consecutive years;

c. is no longer operating in accordance with the cooperative principles and the provisions of this Act; he/she shall send to the chief executive of the cooperative a letter send to the chief executive of the cooperative a letter inquiring whether the cooperative is carrying on business, is in operation, wishes to retain the status of a cooperative or is submitting an annual return.

2) Whether registrar does not, within one month of the date he/she sent a letter in pursuance of sub-section (1), receive an answer to the letter, he/she shall, within 14 days after the expiry of the month, send to the chief executive of the cooperative a letter referring to the letter sent in pursuance of sub-section(1) and stating that:

a. no answer to that letter has been received by him/her; and

b. if an answer is not received to the letter sent under this sub-section within one month from the date it is sent, a notice will be published in the gazette to strike the name of the cooperative off the register and to dissolve the cooperative.

3) Where the registrar:

a. receives an answer from the cooperative that it is not carrying on business or is not operation or does not wish to keep its cooperative status or will not be submitting an annual return; or

b. does not, within one month after the date that he/she sent a letter in pursuance of sub-section(2), receive an answer to that letter;

he/she after consulting the federal cooperatives may publish in the gazette and send to the cooperative a notice that, at the expiry of one month from the date of that notice, the cooperative will, unless cause is shown to the contrary, be struck off the register and the cooperative will be dissolved.

4) At the expiry of the period mentioned in a notice sent pursuant to sub-section(3), the registrar may, unless cause to the contrary is previously shown by the cooperative:

   a. where he/she is satisfied that the cooperative has no assets or liabilities, issue a certificate of dissolution; or

   b. appoint a liquidator to dissolve the cooperative.

5) Where a cooperative fails to furnish a copy of the annual financial statements to its members:

   a. at an annual or special meeting called for that purpose; or

   b. within a period of 8 months after the close of its financial year; the registrar

   c. may require the directors to call a special meeting of the cooperative for the purpose of considering the business transacted during the preceding financial year and for furnishing to the members and to the registrar a copy of the annual financial statement; and

   d. where he/she requires a special meeting to be called pursuant to clause (c), shall determine a time period within which the special meeting is to be called.

6) Where the directors fail to call a special meeting within the time period set out in sub-section (5), the registrar may call the special meeting:

   a. to review the financial position of the cooperative and the members' interests in the cooperative; and

b. to ascertain whether the members desire to continue the cooperative.

7) Where

a. a quorum of members is not present at a special meeting called in pursuance of sub-section(6); or

b. the members fail to pass a resolution to the effect that the cooperatives is to carry on business and that the board must present the financial statements the registrar may appoint a liquidator to dissolve the cooperative, or where the registrar is satisfied that the cooperative has no assets or liabilities, he/she may issue a certificate of dissolution.

47. Dissolution by court order

1) The registrar or an interested person may, after giving the cooperative three months notice of the proposed application, apply to a court for an order dissolving a cooperative, where the cooperative:

a. obtained its registration by mistake or fraud;

b. exists for an illegal purpose;

c. has wilfully, after notice by the registrar violated any of the provisions of this Act or its byelaws;

d. is no longer operating on a cooperative basis.

2) Where an interested person applies in pursuance of this section, he/she give the registrar notice of his/her application and the registrar is entitled to appear and be heard in person or by counsel.

3) Where the court receives an application in pursuance of this section, it may order that the cooperative be dissolved or liquidated and dissolved under the supervision of the registrar.

4) Where the registrar receives an order made in pursuance of sub-section(3), he/she shall

a. where the order is to dissolve the cooperative, issue a certificate of dissolution; or

b. where the order is to liquidate and dissolve the cooperative under the supervision of the registrar, publish a notice in the gazette.

48. Appointment of liquidator

Where a cooperative is to be liquidated and dissolved and no liquidator is appointed by the general body or the court, the registrar may:

a. appoint any person as a liquidator to wind up the affairs of the cooperative; or

b. where he/she is satisfied that the cooperative has no assets and liabilities, issue a certificate of dissolution.

49. Duties of liquidator

On his/her appointment, a liquidator shall:

a. immediately give notice of his/her appointment;

(i) in the case of liquidator not appointed by the registrar, to the registrar; and

(ii) to each claimant and creditor known to the liquidator:

b. immediately publish notice of her/her appointment in the gazette once a week for two consecutive weeks in a newspaper published or distributed in the place where the cooperative has its registered office and take reasonable steps to give notice of the liquidation in every jurisdiction of where the cooperative carries on business;

c. place in the notice mentioned in clause (a) and (b) a provision requiring any person:

(i) indebted to the cooperative, to render an account and pay to the liquidator at the time and place specified any amount owing;

(ii) possessing property of the cooperative, to deliver it to the liquidator at the time and place specified; and

(iii) having a claim against the cooperative, whether liquidated, unliquidated, future or contingent, to present particulars of the claim in writing to the liquidator not later than two months after the first publication of the notice.

d. take into custody and control the property of the cooperative;

e. open and maintain a trust account for the moneys of the cooperative;

f. kept accounts of the moneys of the cooperative received and paid out by him/her;

g. maintain separate lists of the members, creditors and other persons having claims against the cooperative

h. whereat any time he/she determines that the cooperative is unable to pay or adequately provide for the discharge of its obligations, apply to the registrar for directions; and

i. deliver to the registrar, at least once in every six month period after his/her appointment or more often as the registrar may require, financial statements of the cooperative in any form that the liquidator considers proper or that the registrar may require.

50. Powers of liquidator

1) The liquidator may:

a. retain lawyers, accounts, engineers, appraisers and other professional advisors;

b. bring, defend or take part in any civil, criminal or administrative action or proceeding in the name and on behalf of the cooperative;

c. carry on the business of the cooperative as required for an orderly liquidation;

d. sell by public auction or private sale any property of the cooperative;

e. do all acts and execute any documents in the name and on behalf of the cooperative;

f. borrow money on the security of the property of the cooperative;

g. settle or compromise any claims by or against the cooperative; and

h. do all other things that he/she considers necessary for the liquidation of the cooperative and distribution of its property and funds.

2) Where a liquidator has reason to believe that any person has in his/her possession or under his/her control or has concealed, withheld or misappropriated any property of the cooperative, he/she may apply to the court for an order requiring that person to appear before the court at the time and place designated in the order and to be examined.

3) Where the examination mentioned in sub-section(2) discloses that a person has concealed, withheld or misappropriated property of the cooperative, the court may order that person to restore the property or pay compensation to the liquidator on behalf of the cooperative.

4) No liquidator or his/her relatives shall purchase, directly or indirectly, any part of the stock-in-trade, debts or assets of the cooperative.

51. Final account

1) A liquidator shall pay the costs of liquidation out of the property of the cooperative and shall pay or make adequate provision for all claims against the cooperative.

2) After paying or making adequate provision for all claims against the cooperative, the liquidator shall apply to the registrar for approval of his/her final accounts and for permission to distribute in money or in kind the remaining property of the cooperative in accordance with the byelaws.

3) Where the registrar approves the final accounts rendered by a liquidator in pursuance of sub-section(2), he/she shall

   a. issue directions with respect to the custody or disposal of the documents and records of the cooperative; and

   b. discharge the liquidator.

4) Where the registrar discharges a liquidator pursuant to sub-section(3), he/she shall issue a certificate of dissolution.

5) The cooperative ceases to exist on the date shown in the certificate of dissolution, which shall not be latter than twenty four months after appointment of the liquidator.

Chapter – XI

Miscellaneous

52. Enabling provision for different cooperatives

To facilitate appropriate constitution, management and conduct of business in different types of cooperatives, special legal provisions may be enacted and provided for as a separate chapter in this Act.

ANNEXURE-B

National Policy on Cooperatives*

The Need for a National Policy

The role of cooperatives has acquired a new dimension in the changing scenario of globalization and liberalization of Nation's economy. Internal and structural weaknesses of these institutions combined with lack of proper policy support have neutralized their positive impact. There are wide regional imbalances in the development of the cooperatives in the country. This has necessitated the need for a clear-cut national policy on cooperatives to enable sustained development and growth of healthy and self-reliant cooperatives for meeting the sectoral/regional aspirations of the people in consonance with the principles of cooperation. In this connection, it is also imperative to address the issues which require to be attended to by evolving a suitable legislative and policy support to these institutions.

The proposed National Policy on Cooperatives, as follows, is a part of the concerted efforts of the government to provide appropriate policy and legislative support to cooperatives with a view to revitalizing them.

Objective

The objective of the National Policy is to facilitate all round development of the cooperatives in the country. Under this Policy, cooperatives would be provided necessary support, encouragement and assistance, so as to ensure that they work as autonomous, self-reliant and democratically managed institutions accountable to their members and make a significant contribution to the national economy, particularly in areas which require people's participation and

* For further details see the document in NCUI, ICA Library.

community efforts. This is all the more important in view of the fact that still a sizeable segment of the population in the country is below poverty line and the cooperatives are the only appropriate mechanism to lend support to this section of the people.

The National Policy on Cooperatives to this seek to achieve:

- Ensuring functioning of the cooperatives based on basic cooperative values and principles as enshrined in the declaration of the International Cooperative Alliance Congress, 1995;
- Revitalization of the cooperative structure particularly in the sector of agricultural credit;
- Reduction of regional imbalance through provision of support measure by the Central Government/State Government, particularly in the underdeveloped and cooperatively underdeveloped States/regions;
- Strengthening of the Cooperative Education and Training and Human Resource Development for professionalisation of the management of the Cooperatives;
- Greater participation of members in the management of cooperatives and promoting the concept of user members;
- Amendment/removal of provisions in cooperative laws providing for the restrictive regulatory regime;
- Evolving a system of integrated cooperatives structure by entrusting the federations predominantly the role of promotion, guidance information system, etc. towards their affiliate members and potential members;
- Evolving a system of inbuilt mechanism in Cooperative legislation to ensure timely conduct of general body meetings, elections and audit of cooperative societies;

- Ensuring that the benefits of the cooperatives' endeavour reach the poorer seçtions of the society and encouraging the participation of such sections and women in management of cooperatives.

Policy

The Government of India in consultation and collaboration with the State Governments hereby enuciates the following:

(i) While holding the values and principles of cooperation, it recognizes the cooperatives as autonomous associations of persons, united voluntarily to meet their common economic, social and cultural needs and aspirations through jointly owned and democratically controlled enterprises;

(ii) Upholds the preservation of the distinct identity of cooperatives, its values and principles by providing an appropriate environment and taking the required administrative and legislative measures;

(iii) Recognizes cooperatives as a distinct economic sector and an integral component of the socioeconomic system of the country and an effective and potential instrument of socio-economic development. It considers them as essentially community initiatives for harnessing people's creative power, autonomous, democratically managed, decentralized, need-based and sustainable economic enterprises. Cooperative will, however, remain the preferred instrument of execution of the public policy especially in the rural area;

(iv) The regulatory role of the Government will be mainly limited to the conduct of timely elections, audit of the cooperative societies, and measures to safeguard the interest of the members and other stakeholders in the cooperatives. There shall, however, be no interference in the management and working of the cooperatives. The Government recognizes the apolitical nature of cooperatives;

(v) Reiterates and reinforces its commitment to the cause of the SC/ST, women and other weaker sections of the Society and their development through the cooperatives. Wherever members belonging to women or Scheduled Castes/ Scheduled Tribes and other backward castes want to have their exclusive societies provided they find a socioeconomic reason to form such a society, encouragement and assistance will be provided by the Government. Cooperative Societies, if they so decide, can provide for the representation of such category of persons in their byelaws which they are competent to frame;

(vi) Accepts the need to phase out its share holdings/equity participation in the cooperatives. It shall, however, endeavour and extend appropriate support for improving financial viability and resource mobilization by harnessing local savings and adequate refinance facility, and to the possible extent providing a policy framework to ensure that there is no discrimination against the cooperatives in the mature relating to resource mobilization to attain financial viability. The cooperatives shall be enabled to set up holding companies/ subsidiaries, enter into strategic partnership, venture into futuristic areas like insurance, food processing and information technology etc., and shall be independent to take the financial decisions in the interest of the members and in furtherance of their stated objects;

(vii) Recongizes the role of the Government in ensuring that the benefits of liberalization and globalization in the emerging economic environment are extended to the cooperatives in equal measure through suitable fiscal policies and pledges to provide support and protection to the cooperative movement through suitably designed investment programemss with a view to providing the cooperatives a level playing field vis-à-vis other competing enterprises especially in the field of agro-processing and marketing;

(viii) Recognizes the need for more effective regulation of cooperatives operating in the financial sector and accepting public deposits;

(ix) Also recognizes the need for incorporating special provision in the Cooperative Societies Act with regard to banking, housing, real estate development, processing, manufactures cooperatives, infrastructure development, etc;

(x) Recognizes the need to provide preferential treatment, as far as possible, to the cooperatives engaged in areas such as credit, labour, consumer, services, housing, development of SC/ST and women and development of emerging areas as well as sectors requiring people's participation especially in rural areas;

(xi) Undertakes to devise and execute suitable programmes and schemes to build and develop cooperative institutions in the cooperative under-developed States/regions with particular reference to the North Eastern States including Sikkim;

(xii) Recognizes the need to support the cooperative movement to develop human resources, cooperative education and training, appropriate technologies and infrastructural facilities so as to promote professional management in cooperatives particularly at the primary level, for their greater functional and operational efficiency. It may also include the introduction of cooperatives as a curriculum vita at school level;

(xiii) Undertakes to initiate structural reforms in order to improve the functioning of the cooperatives at various levels to ensure greater efficiency and viability. These may include steps to activate idle membership, enhance member participation and involvement, provision of multi cooperatives approach, ensure timely conduct of general body meetings and elections, provide for effective audit, devise suitable mechanism for rehabilitation of the sick societies particularly in the processing sector, expedite winding up of defunct societies; and providing legal framework for voluntary winding up of cooperatives;

(xiv) Undertakes to bestow autonomy to follow appropriate personnel policies including those relating to recruitment, promotions and other such matters with due emphasis on quality and transparency;

(xv) Undertakes to introduce the required electoral reforms through legislative measures. Elections to the cooperative societies should be held through an independent authority like the State Election Commission; and

(xvi) Also undertakes to take other such measures as would be required for efficient and healthy growth of the cooperative movement.

Plan of Action

A plan of action of implementation of the policy shall be formulated and pursued with adequate budgetary support by the Government of India, state governments and other concerned agencies including federal/national level cooperative organizations in a time bound manner.

Conclusion

The Government of India trusts that the enunciation of this statement of policy on Cooperatives aimed at professionalisatoin and democratization of their operations will facilitate the development of cooperatives as self-reliant and economically viable organizations, providing their members improved access to the economies of scale, offsetting various risk elements, safeguarding them against market imperfections and bestowing the advantages of collective action.

And further trusts that the above statement of policy would ensure enduring autonomy and lasting viability to them as democratically owned, self-reliant enterprises, responsible and accountable to their members and to a larger public interest.

ANNEXURE-C

COMMITTEES AND COMMISSIONS ON COOPERATION - MAJOR RECOMMENDATIONS*

Maclagen Committee Report (1914)

The Committee on Cooperation was set up in October 1914 with E.D. Maclagen as its Chairman.

Recommendations

- Numbering not less than 10, individuals combine together as they are unable to obtain credit individually.
- Real security consists not of material assets of members, but their ability and desire to use credit productively and to repay loans out of profits made. Productive use of credit and moral pressure on co-members to duly repay would ensure loan security.
- Societies to be cooperative and business like, small in size.
- One vote per member, transparency of business transactions, development of thrift and obtaining maximum capital from savings.
- Period of the loan be fixed based on purpose of loan and the circumstances of the borrower.
- Rates of interest to be initially substantial, although lower than that on credit from moneylenders.
- Efforts increase deposits both from members and non-members.
- Primary society would be financed by Central Coop. Financing Agencies, either through the RCS Office on his endorsement,

*Government of India, Ministry of Agriculture, Report of the High Powered Committee on Cooperatives, May, 2009, pp. 74-95

or on the recommendation of a Union of which primary societies are members and exercise control on errant societies.

- Maximum borrowing limit of the society be annually fixed.
- Obtaining share capital in instalments excellent means of inculcating thrift and providing capital.
- Interest rates not to be reduced until reserve funds have reached substantial figure.
- Frequent audit by higher cooperative institutions with Government Audit once in 2 or 3 years, with cost being met by the societies.
- Registrar should ensure supervision and control of primary societies without assuming detailed direction.
- To meet their deposits due, Banks must equilibrate their finances with care, providing for retention of adequate fluid resources.
- Need for Registrars staff to be increased and agriculture and industry in the provinces to be coordinated under one head; appointment of a Development Commissioner and a Cooperative Adviser also recommended.
- For coordination and control, a strong apex or provincial bank needed.

Royal Commission on Agriculture in India (1928)

The Royal Commission on Agriculture, appointed to make recommendations for improvement of agriculture and promotion of welfare and prosperity of the rural population, submitted its report in April 1928.

Recommendations

- Main activities of the cooperative movement must continue

to be directed to expansion of the rural credit system; defects pointed out by the Committee on Cooperation 1914-1915 still persisted and although the number of societies has increased there was no qualitative improvement.

- Need for member education stressed.
- As in Europe where strong Central Federations undertake the work of organization and inspection, such supervising Unions or Provincial Unions, which are efficient, could be assisted by the Government.
- Role of the Registrar to be not merely a registering officer, but to provide supervision, assistance, counsel and control.
- To ensure continuity, Registrar not to be transferred for a minimum period of 5 years.
- More Government contribution in backward tracts and for certain activities such as irrigation, consolidation of land holdings etc.
- Importance should be attached to every phase of activity; the term rural reconstruction expressed more accurately the nature of activities within the movement.
- Establishment of land mortgage banks with guarantee of interest on its debentures by Government under the Cooperative Act to meet the requirements of the cultivator other than small needs.
- Central Organization for control of debenture issue and measures for financial disciplines.
- Single purpose cooperatives by and large favoured; need for extension of cooperative principles in fields other than cooperative credit; cooperative input and sale societies also identified as areas for development.

Cooperative Planning Committee (1945)

Arising as a result of the recommendation of the 14th Conference of Registrars of Cooperative Societies held in 1944, the Cooperative Planning Committee constituted in January 1945 under the chairmanship of R.G. Saraiya to draw up a plan of cooperative development in the country, submitted its report in November 1945. The Committee felt that supply of credit touches only one aspect of the life of the cultivator and the activities of Primary Cooperative Societies should be so extended as to cover the whole of his life.

Recommendations

- The Multipurpose Society should serve as a Centre for general economic improvement. Apart from financing crop production, it should act as an agent for sale of produce to the nearest cooperative marketing organization; supply farmers with their production needs and dairy consumption requirements; serve as milk collecting station for the nearest dairy and provision of veterinary services, maintain agriculture machinery to be jointly used by members and encourage subsidiary occupations by its members.
- Membership of such societies should be a minimum of 50 and confined to an area of operation, which would ensure adequate business as well as efficient supervision and control.
- Except in cases where unlimited liability has been successful, the society should be one of limited liability.
- The Committee also dealt in detail with cooperatives in the areas of animal husbandry and fisheries, agricultural marketing and processing, agricultural credit, labour and civil construction, consumers, urban credit, housing societies, women and cooperation, cooperative administration and education training and research.

- Linking of agricultural credit with marketing. Credit societies should give loans on the condition that the borrowing member would sell the marketable surplus through his primary society to the nearest marketing society of the area.

All India Rural Credit Survey Committee (1951)

The All India Rural Credit Survey Committee was appointed in 1951 and submitted its report in 1954.

Recommendations

- Large parts of the country were not covered by cooperatives. Even in areas where mem-bership existed, bulk of credit requirement (75.2%) was met from other sources.
- Non-economic causes for the failure of the cooperative movement basically structural and functional, low educational levels and lack of training. Multi-purpose Society had not made any significant difference.
- Location of both power and finance continues to be largely urban and hence more respon-sive to urban than rural interest; cooperative in danger from various vested interests.
- Integrated scheme of Rural Credit based on State partnership including financial partner-ship in cooperatives; training with a rural bias.
- Caution against state interference in day to day working. While societies at the rural base should become fully cooperative by process of replacing share capital, partnerships at higher levels have to be retained till base level societies develop sufficient strength.
- Setting up of a National Agricultural Credit Long Term Operations Fund and National Ag-ricultural Credit Stabilization Fund to be reviewed at the end of 5 years, responsibility for which would be with the Reserve Bank.

- Administrative and other matters including training.
- Creation of the State Bank of India.
- Establishment of a Central Land Mortgage Bank in each State with more than 51% of State share capital.
- Apex Cooperative Marketing Federations.
- Licenses to be issued on a priority basis to cooperative processing plants.
- State plans for rationalizing and strengthening Central Cooperative Banks.
- District Marketing Societies on territorial or commodity basis with at least 51% State Govt. share capital and suitable technical staff, PACS with reasonably large membership and share capital and covering groups of villages; detailed observations with regard to the nature of liability, deposit, reserve, loan operations of PACS; establishment of primary land mortgage banks and primary marketing societies located at important mandis or at taluka centers after due consideration of the conditions of each area.
- Audit continue to be in the hands of govt. and be strengthened on a high priority; adoption of uniform standards of audit classification on an All India basis.

Committee on Cooperative Law (1957)

Appointed under the chairmanship of S.T. Raja in 1956 to evolve a simple law for cooperatives, the Committee submitted its Report in May 1957.

Recommendations

- Increasing decentralization of powers of Registrar.
- Persons, on whom powers of the Registrar could be conferred, should work under the Registrar.

- Registration of societies to conform to economic interests of members, social justice and sound business; amendment to bylaws also in accordance.
- Unlimited liability in case of societies.
- Amalgamation to be in accordance with wishes and interests of members.
- Membership not to be open to firms, partnerships and companies.
- Nominal or associate members to have NO voting powers or share in profit of societies.
- One man - one vote and no proxy.
- Ceiling on individual shareholding (Rs 5,000).
- Powers of the General Body specifically laid down in the Model Bill; provision for a smaller body of delegates where membership is too large and widespread.
- Any transfer of assets or property by members without previous consent of the society to be void, notwithstanding any law in force.
- State partnership, preferably to be direct.
- Contributions to reserve fund out of profits to be not less than 25%; contributory provident fund not to be used in business.
- All states should set up Cooperative Tribunals.

Report of Sir Malcom Darling (1957)

After studying the functioning of cooperatives in India, Sir Malcom Darling was not in favour of the new large sized society pattern, mainly due to its large area of operation.

Recommendations

- The area of operation of a society should not normally exceed a distance of two miles from its headquarter village.
- Societies undertaking banking should not be allowed to undertake trading, since banking and trading did not go together.
- Small societies should not be amalgamated without the full and free consent of a large majority of their members.
- The old name Thrift and Credit Society should be restored and scrupulously insisted upon at the time of registering a rural credit society at the primary level.

National Development Council Resolution (1958)

Highlights of the Resolution

- Cooperatives to be organized on a village basis and primary responsibility on Panchayat.
- Various programmes for increasing agricultural production to be carried out through cooperatives.
- Village societies to be federated through Unions and also become members of Marketing Societies.
- National savings movement to utilize cooperatives as primary agencies in rural areas.
- Development of marketing societies, on the basis of careful surveys of marketable surplus in different areas, emphasized.
- Emphasis on training.

Working Group on Cooperative Policy (1958)

This Group was appointed by the Government of India with Damle to consider the administrative and organizational arrangements needed for the implementation of 1958 Resolution of the National Development Council.

Recommendations

- The village cooperative should be organized on the basis of village community as the primary unit and include within itself all the families living in the village, whether they are cultivators, agricultural labourers, artisans or other groups such as fishermen etc. and it should provide to them not only credit, but also agricultural requisites and consumer goods.
- It would be more advisable not to combine the credit function which was of primary importance to all the people in the village with such other functions in which only a few people might be interested or which might involve long term investment or financial risks. Thus a village might have, in addition to village multi-purpose society one or more cooperatives for specific tasks and specific interests.
- The Group recommended two patterns of organizations: one being the organization of credit societies each of which would ordinarily have the village as the area of operation and in any case not cover a population of more than 1000 and the other being the organization of credit unions for a group of villages to undertake credit activities, the village societies in such cases being expected to deal with other activities.

These recommendations were communicated by the Government of India to the State Governments in May, 1959 for cooperative revitalization.

Working Group on Cooperative Farming (1959)

The Working Group on Cooperative Farming set up in 1959 under the chairmanship of S. Nijalingappa was to examine and suggest measures for promoting joint farming cooperative societies.

Recommendations

- Flexibility in organization, voluntary membership and more than one society in a village, if required.
- Decision making power to vest with General Body; if required Sub-Committees for different subjects, where membership is large.
- Model bylaws prescribed.
- Finance from Land Mortgage Banks for long-term credit (necessary amendments in Co-operative Act for this purpose), medium-term credit from CCBs against landed security , short-term credit based on repaying capacity.
- Initially Government to participate in share capital, which may be retired over a 10 year period through creation of share redemption fund or members contribution.
- Assistance under various Government schemes, as well as extension services should be made available.
- Managerial subsidy for 3 years.
- Society to be allowed to advance loans for consumption needs; mutual aid fund and chit fund to be created for this purpose.
- Education and training for ensuring success stressed.

Committee on Cooperative Credit (1960)

The Committee on Cooperative Credit headed by V.L. Mehta was appointed in September 1959 and submitted its report in May 1960.

Recommendations

- Cooperatives should strengthen themselves financially and otherwise and extend their range of credit and distribution operations..

- Promotion of viable units.
- Government contribution to share capital on a matching basis; specified subsidy for a period not more than 5 years and subscription by govt. to a special bad debt reserve.
- Loans to tenant cultivators, ceiling on credit limit to ensure needs of small and medium cultivators are met, short-term loans on production of two sureties from fellow members.
- Detailed guidelines for determining perks of cooperative banks.
- Share capital of government to be conditional on minimum contribution being raised by members over a specified period; partnership of State at primary level to be indirect.
- Nominees of the Govt. or CCB would not have veto rights and Govt. should not interfere in the day to day working.
- At the village level, only one institutional agency for supply of credit viz., the cooperative.
- Arrangements for linking credit with marketing should be strengthened. Cooperative Marketing Societies should be permitted to make outright purchases from the producers.
- Constitution and strengthening of the Agricultural Credit Stabilization Fund: Credit on the basis of repaying capacity to be provided to land less, tenants, marginal or sub-marginal farmers.
- Government to make outright contributions at fixed percentages for additional finance for agricultural production. This would not include jewel loans. The contribution would go to a special bad debt reserve, distinct from bad debt reserve created out of profits.
- State to provide initial assistance for cooperatives, but not to interfere in internal management.

- Special concessions to be given to scheduled castes and scheduled tribes.

Working Group Panchayats and Cooperatives (1961)

Set up under the chairmanship of S.D. Mishra to suggest measures for cooperatives and panchayats to perform their respective roles in coordination, the Committee submitted its Report in October 1961.

Recommendations

- To organize lectures by leaders, help increase membership deposits and share capital and to ensure that loans are utilized properly and repaid in time.
- To provide accommodation and also land to cooperatives for godowns etc. and processing licenses to cooperatives preferentially; Panchayat to deposit its funds with the village cooperative.
- Help in member education.
- All commercial agricultural functions to be run by the cooperative.
- Close coordination for drawing up village agricultural production plans and credit requirements.
- All economic and technical matters to be coordinated at Zila Parishad/Panchayat level.
- Work programmes of panchayats to be executed through labour cooperatives or community effort.

Report of the Study Team on Cooperative Training (1961)

Appointed under the chairmanship of S.D. Mishra, the Committee submitted its report in 1961.

Recommendations

- District and State Cooperative Unions to be strengthened to undertake cooperative training and education.

- Schools to teach cooperation as also universities, rural institutes and teacher training institutes .
- Students to be enabled to be members of school cooperatives, if necessary amending age provisions of Cooperative Acts.
- Member education to be peripatetic and based on the problems of the cooperatives.
- Specialized courses for institutional and departmental personnel should be organized including courses in Banking, Industrial Cooperation, Consumers Cooperation etc. All courses should have more of practical training and use new teaching techniques and audio-visual aids.
- Field studies and research programmes to be undertaken through universities, institutes and institutions, cooperative unions, rural economic division of RBI and the National Board of Cooperative Training.
- Preparation of pamphlets in local languages, text books, films, departmental manuals, cooperative journals, publishing success stories and case studies by NCUI and SCU (expenditure to be shared by Government).
- Setting up of a National Board for Cooperative Training and NCUI to coordinate member education programme.
- Cooperative institute for advanced study and research to be set up.
- 1% of net profit of cooperatives to be contributed to SCU for cooperative education and training purposes.

Committee on Consumers Cooperatives (1961)

Set up by the National Cooperative Development and Ware Housing Board under the chairmanship of P. Natesan, the Committee submitted its report in 1961.

Recommendations

- Setting up of consumer stores in larger towns and cities, service cooperatives to function as consumer stores at village level, with special attention to viability.
- As a rule, avoidance of trading activities along with banking.
- Initial government share capital, to be retired within a period of 10-15 years.
- Trading against cash.
- Creation of Price Fluctuation Fund.
- Rebates to members to be credited to share accounts.
- Incentives to Managers through commission on sales.
- Managerial subsidy.
- Concurrent audit; audit fee to be linked to profit instead of turnover.
- Sales-tax exemption on sales to affiliated primaries.
- Government requirements preferentially met through consumer cooperatives.

Committee on Cooperative Processing (1961)

Appointed by the National Cooperative Development and Warehousing Board under the chairmanship of R.G. Saraiya, the Committee submitted its report in 1961.

Recommendations

- Linking of credit with processing, processing and distributive institutions stressed.
- Proper planning.
- Preferential licensing policy.

- Members to be producers; membership to be opened to Primary Credit Societies in area of operation to facilitate recovery of crop loans.
- Credit Guarantee Scheme of GOI to be extended to cooperative processing units.
- Preferential treatment in case of taxation.

Committee on Taccavi Loans and Cooperative Credit (1962)

The NDC in 1958 had recommended making Taccavi Loans and other facilities through cooperatives to encourage increase in its membership. Progress was, however, not appreciable and GOI appointed a Committee in July 1961 to examine the whole question of implementation of the policy.

Recommendations

- Panchayats would prepare production plans which would be implemented through cooperatives.
- Cooperatives would be associated in preparation of plans.
- Cooperatives would be the institutional agency for credit to agriculturists, except in certain cases involving financial risks or delayed returns where govt. would continue direct finance.
- Government funds should supplement the resources of cooperatives and govt. budget provisions should continue.
- Cooperative dues be given priority over Taccavi loans.
- Cooperatives adopt system of credit based on repaying capacity and adequate security.
- Distress taccavi loans be granted by financially strong cooperatives, which would function purely on agency basis.
- Cooperative banking structure be rationalized.

- Land mortgage banking structure be a federal one with central land mortgage bank at state level and primary land mortgage banks at lower level. PLMB may have branches at Taluka Block Headquarters. PLMDB may be given power to sanction loans up to certain limit.
- GOI to expedite Refinance Corporation for agriculture to help CLMBs in long term resources.
- Cooperatives to continue to charge economic lending rate on short and medium term loans.

Report of Committee on Cooperative Administration (1963)

Set up in 1963 under the chairmanship of Vaikunthlal Mehta, the Committee was to make recommendations regarding staffing at various levels, criteria for determining staff strength, training of staff and procedures for recruitment.

Recommendations

- IAS officers to be inducted as Registrars, taking account of suitability and with sufficient.
- Orientation of the Cooperative Department; continuity through appointment for at least 3 years, preferably 4-5 years to be ensured.
- Joint Registrars for audit, banking and credit, cooperative marketing and processing (exclusively for cooperative processing, if sufficiently developed) industrial cooperatives and cooperative stores.
- Technical Experts to be taken on loan from concerned departments.
- Divisional Offices of cooperatives to have the same jurisdiction as Revenue Department.

- Functions of Divisional Offices and statutory and financial powers (except those reserved for being exercised only by the Registrar) to cover district offices in the Division.
- Cooperative enterprises of all kinds to be under administrative control of the Registrar; where such powers given to any other department, officers of Cooperative Department be posted to supervise societies and advise on cooperative aspects.
- Audit to remain the statutory duty of the Registrar and separate Audit Wing under a Chief Auditor to be set up.
- While not favouring deputation of departmental staff, on requisition by a society, a panel of names may be provided by Registrar, with ultimate selection by the Society Board.
- The President of the Board of Directors should be entitled to record his views on the work of the government official in his confidential report.
- Recommendations on pay scales, recruitment and training of officers of Cooperative Department.
- Promotion of federal bodies and consideration of transfer to them of statutory powers of the Registrar.

Second Working Group on Industrial Cooperatives (1963)

Set up under the chairmanship of B.P. Patel, the Group submitted its report in May 1963.

Recommendations

- Banks to be selected and developed for industrial loans.
- Federations of Industrial Cooperatives to be set up at important market centers on a single or multi-industry basis.
- At least one State level Industrial Cooperative Federation.
- Revitalization.

- State Acts to be suitably amended for needs of Industrial Cooperatives.
- Government share capital loans to members; government share capital in Federal Cooperatives.
- New District Industrial Cooperative Banks where considerable concentration of small industrial units; SCB and CCBs at district level also be enabled to finance Industrial Cooperatives.
- List of areas in which SBI expected to operate to be drawn up.

Conference of State Ministers of Cooperation (1964)

The Conference, after considering the issue of viability laid down the following minimum criteria of viability of a primary society:

- Appoint a full time paid Secretary.
- Set up a regular office in a building owned or hired.
- Contribute to statutory and other reserves.
- Pay a reasonable dividend.
- Programme for organization of viable societies involved three stages, viz.
- The formulation of viability criteria by State Governments.
- Survey to locate viable and potentially viable units.
- Drawing up of a programme of amalgamation of non-viable units and liquidation of defunct societies.

The entire programme of reorganization was expected to be completed by 1966-67 and to bring down the number of primary societies in the country to 1.20 lakhs.

Mirdha Committee on Cooperatives (1965)

The Committee was to lay down standards to determine

genuineness of cooperative societies and suggest measures to weed out non-genuine societies; to review existing cooperative laws and practices to eliminate vested interest; and suggest measures to overcome factors inhibiting self-reliance and self-regulation in the cooperative movement.

Recommendations

The Committee:

- Endorsed the cooperative principles.
- The Registrar in consultation with apex institutions to lay down detailed conditions for ensuring minimum performance level such as; minimum membership, minimum share capital before registration, promoters to be from different families etc; scrutiny before registration and careful watch after.
- Targets to be dependant on financial resources and administrative preparedness.
- All members to be admitted except moneylenders in credit societies and traders in marketing societies. Similarly, contractors, transporters etc. not to be admitted to labour cooperatives, transport cooperatives respectively.
- Safeguards suggested for cooperative housing societies.
- Open membership and provision for appeal against refusal to admit a member.
- Sanction of loans to managing committee members or their relatives and default in repay-ment by them to be put up to general body for information.
- General Body to decide on number of terms a person may hold office in the Management Committee and number of societies. However, conventions should be evolved regarding these.

- Elections to be held at least with a gap of 2 years to enable committee members to work.
- Co-option of general members in sub-committees to encourage involvement.
- Audit arrangements, dates for submission to be fixed and committee members to be answerable for non-compliance.
- Regular General Body meetings for considering accounts and elections; committee members to be answerable for non-compliance.
- Federal structure to be strictly followed and individual members normally not to be allowed in central apex or national societies.
- All important interests to be represented in Management Committee.
- Government nomination not to exceed one third of committee members or three whichever is less and only government servants should be nominated; code of conduct to be evolved for nominated Directors.
- Audit, to be objective, should be entrusted to a government agency independent of the Registrar.
- Federal cooperatives to take responsibility for supervision; governments may strengthen apex societies for this purpose.
- State partnership in cooperatives to continue; Long Term Operations Fund to be strengthened.
- Overall assessment of credit requirement to be made.
- Cooperative institutions to be allowed to raise deposits and a system of ensuring or guar-anteeing deposits be evolved to build up public confidence.

- National Cooperative Bank through which all finance to cooperatives by Central Govt. and RBI may flow.
- Cooperative education emphasized; NCUI and SCU to be responsible for training institutions; societies may contribute to Cooperative Education Fund out of their net profits.

ICA Commission on Cooperative Principles (1966)

The Report of the Commission on Cooperative Principles set up in 1964 under the chairmanship of D.G. Karve, to examine the need for reformulation of the cooperative principles was accepted by the 23rd Congress of the ICA in 1966.

Recommendations

The report identified the six Principles of Cooperation.

All India Rural Credit Review Committee (1969)

Also known as the Venkatappaiah Committee, the Committee submitted its report in July 1969.

Recommendations

- Agricultural Credit Corporations to be set up in States.
- SCB to play major role in rectifying deficiencies in cooperative credit and various steps taken to strengthen SCBs.
- SCB through its branches to finance PACS, where CCB is inoperative and similarly, CCB to finance cultivators where PACS dormant.
- Appropriate staffing and upgradation through training.
- Special grants by State Government to cooperative banks for employment of staff and to write off irrecoverable debts in certain cases.
- Supersession of management and appointment of Administrative Officer in special cases.

- Amalgamation of Banks where required.
- Rehabilitation of weak Central Banks.
- Promotion of viable units at the primary level so as to ensure that area of operation is not too large for the cultivators' convenience.
- Efforts to convert all PACS to limited liability.
- Reactivation of dormant societies or their liquidation.
- State government to contribute additional sums to share capital of PACS where levels of non credit business warrant this.
- Managerial subsidies to societies which employ a full time paid Secretary.
- Data verification of land records etc. to ensure reliability of credit finance.
- Scales of finance to be fixed up and credit to consist of two components viz., cash and kind.
- Recoveries to be tightened up.
- Supersession of management where Society affairs are unsatisfactory and Central Bank having a say in the management until a fresh elected Board is in position.
- State Acts and Rules to incorporate provisions for defaulters to be disqualified from continuing on Board of Directors.
- Financing of defaulters to be barred, those unable to repay on account of crop failure to be provided with conversion facilities or in certain cases to be granted extensions.
- Detailed guidelines for structure and resources of LDBs and lending policies and procedures were laid down.
- Special care to be taken for financing small cultivators. Small Farmers Development Agency to be established in selected districts for this purpose.

- RBI Act to be amended to provide for the constitution of Agricultural Credit Board, which would function through separate Standing Committees and may also deal with non-agricultural aspects of rural credit and all relevant aspects of cooperative credit.
- Provisions of the Banking Regulations Act may be gradually extended to select agricultural credit societies.
- To cover rural electrification aspect, a Rural Electrification Fund to be administered by a Rural Electrification Corporation may be set up.
- The Committee also made recommendations with regard to medium term finance for agricul-ture, credit for animal husbandry, fisheries and other activities, and credit for marketing.
- Grant of pledge loans by marketing societies to members to be continued subject to certain safeguards.
- Need for qualified staff at all levels and appropriate training was emphasized; a study team was proposed to examine and design training courses and determine the magnitude of training required at all levels.
- Training should emphasize practical aspects of working.
- Member education was also emphasized.

National Commision on Agriculture (1971)

The Committee examined in depth the organizational structure for rural credit with special reference to small and marginal farmers.

Recommendations

The Committee recommended the establishment of Farmers Service Societies (FSS) to serve through an integrated credit service to the large number of small and marginal cultivators and provide for meeting all their needs. The FSS could be sponsored by a commercial bank or could form part of the Cooperative Credit System.

Group Headed by Shri Ta.Pa

The Group during the same period examined the most appropriate institutional credit structure for rural areas.

Recommendations

The Group suggested that only the viable multi-purpose, professionally managed cooperative society, organized on the lines of FSS would fulfil the requirements of the rural areas.

Banking Commission (1972)

The Banking Commission set up in 1969 under the chairmanship of R.G. Saraiya to review the working of cooperative banks and recommend coordinated development of commercial and cooperative banks and to review the existing legislative enactment relating to commercial and cooperative banking, submitted its report in 1972.

Recommendations

- Primary credit societies to be so strengthened to enable them to function as Rural Banks. Societies which are potentially viable can be converted to Rural Banks with technical as-sistance from Central Bank/SCB and where these are weak from Commercial Banks.
- Rural Cooperative Banks to have 'Associate Members' who can avail themselves of facilities of the Bank, but will not have voting rights or receive patronage dividends.
- Rural Banks to be supervised by Parent Bank and Reserve Bank.

- Resources for share capital contribution may be made available from National Agricultural Credit Long-term Operations Fund.
- First priority in establishing Rural Banks be given to well run PACS. Special legislation for this purpose and appropriate amendments to cooperative laws to be made.
- Flexibility to Cooperative Banks as in the case of Commercial Banks.
- Diversification of farming essential; hence primary units to be functionally equipped to provide credit for all productive purposes to farmers.
- Real as well as financial assets should be accepted as security.
- Supervision of credit through provision of specialized services for this purpose by Central/SCB, if necessary, suitably subsidized by Government initially.
- Guarantee for financing small and marginal farmers under the Schemes of the Credit Guarantee Corporation.
- Removal of impediments to take action against defaulters.
- As far as possible entire credit should be from a single agency
- Coordination machinery to be set up.
- Deposit Insurance Scheme should be extended to Cooperative Banks.
- Cooperative credit be transferred to the Union/Concurrent list.
- Establishment of National Cooperative Bank not favoured.
- Strong case for combining Agricultural Refinance Corporation and Agricultural Finance Corporation.
- Establishment of Urban Cooperative Banks be encouraged.

Working Group on Cooperation for the Fifth Five Year Plan (1973)

Translated the viability criteria into concrete terms to mean a minimum credit business of Rs 2 lakh (by way of outstanding short term agricultural loans). In May 1976 the Reserve Bank of India suggested to the State Government that a normal cropped area of 2000 hectares of land should be able to provide the minimum business of Rs 2 lakhs as envisaged.

Commitee on Integration of Cooperative Credit Institutions (1976)

Set up in 1975 to study the feasibility of integrating the long term and short term structure of the cooperative movement, the RK Hazari Committee submitted its report in 1976.

Recommendations

- Need for proper linkage between production and investment credit to intensify modernization of agriculture and rectify imbalances in the credit structure.
- Commercial and cooperative credit can jointly play an important role in agricultural finance.
- Compartmentalised approach means the farmer has to approach different agencies for his needs. Public sector agencies are a specialized class of borrowers and LDB cannot lend to them.
- Integration of credit functions between the two wings was felt necessary, for the cooperative credit structure to play an effective role.
- A 3-tier structure at the State, District and Primary level was suggested. A District Cooperative Development Bank (DCDB) at the district level and State Cooperative

Development Bank at the State level (SCDB) through transfer of staff, assets, and liabilities of the DCCB and PLDB at the district level to the newly constituted DCDB and similarly those of the SCB and SLDB at the state level. At the primary level, the process of reorganization and strengthening of PACs to be simultaneously undertaken.

- Gradual decentralization of sanctioning powers.
- Secretaries Cadre Fund to be created and maintained at the SCDB for caderisation of PACs and a permanent cadre of officials at senior and middle levels for the SCDB and DCDB.
- System of Farmers' passbooks to be introduced.
- Group guarantees, where Hypothecation not possible.
- GEHAN to be a new form of security.

Committee on Urban Cooperative Banks (1978)

The Committee was set up in 1978 under the chairmanship of Madhava Das.

Recommendations

- There is a need to stop the practice of primary credit societies commencing banking business without first obtaining licence from RBI.
- Primary credit societies should not be allowed to use the word "bank", "banker" and "banking" as a part of their name to enable the public to distinguish between such societies and banking institutions coming under the purview of B.R. Act, 1949.
- Corresponding legislative amendments required to give effect to these recommendations.
- Existing primary credit societies may be allowed a maximum period of 4 years from the date of coming into force of the

amended provisions of the B.R.Act, 1949. During the intervening period, till such amendments are carried out in the statute, the societies should either reach the level of prescribed viability standards to qualify for the licence or take suitable steps to go out of the purview of B.R.Act, 1949.

Committee to Review Arrangements for Institutional Credit for Agriculture and Rural Development (1981)

The CRAFICARD, under the chairmanship of B. Sivaraman was to review the ARDC, to examine the feasibility of integrating the long-term and medium-term credit structure and to examine the 2-tier vs 3-tier credit system, the role of the AFC and the RBI, submitted its report in January 1981.

Recommendations

- No single pattern feasible for the entire country.
- Farmers Service Societies and LAMPS to be developed.
- Reorganisation drive for societies, which would be single contact point for all types of credit including other rural producers such as artisans, craftsmen, agricultural labour etc.
- Categories of membership: Weaker sections and others.
- Deposit mobilization to be taken up by PACs.
- SCB and CCBs to create a Primary Cooperatives Development Fund.
- Exemptions to defaulters to be completely stopped.
- Rate of interest to be high and a rebate of 2-3% allowed for timely repayment.
- Publishing list of defaulters to act as a deterrent for default.
- Training to be emphasized and planned.

- RRBs to be given preferential licensing in rural areas.
- NABARD to be set up and to take over the work of ARDC and different depts. of the RBI concerned with rural credit.
- A 2-tier structure may exist in the smaller states and UTs, while a 3-tier structure may be the general pattern for the larger states.
- Suggestion of the Hazari Committee for PACs to channel long term funds accepted.
- However desirable to have more than one organization for different purposes working in coordination.
- GOS may seek prior approval of RBI before dissolution of Boards of cooperatives.
- SCBs to use surplus funds to finance processing activities; enter into consortium arrangements with commercial banks.
- Differential rates of interest to be permitted for small ahd large farmers.
- LDBs to be permitted all kinds of term loans including composite loans.
- NAC(LTO) Fund and NAC(Stabilization) Fund to be taken over by the NABARD.

Committee on Democratization and Professionalization of Cooperative Management (1985)

The Committee with Ardhanareeswaran as Chairman has examined various State Cooperative Acts and made the following observations:

- The existing Cooperative Societies Act contain provisions which militate against the democratic character and the autonomy of cooperatives.

- Over the years, the Registrar has acquired undue powers in respect of management decisions of the cooperatives, which should be curtailed.
- The role of the Registrar should be made more positive and the should be looked upon as a development agent.
- The federal cooperative societies should play a more active part in the developmental functions relating to promotion, organization, proper functioning and growth of the affiliated cooperative societies.
- The changing complexities of member management, human resource development, financial management have necessitated availability of professional assistance to cooperatives through adequate trained and professional paid staff on appropriate terms working under the general guidance of a democratically elected body.

Committee on Structure and Role of National Cooperative Societies (1987)

The Committee was set up under the chairmanship of B.Venkatappiah to assess the performance of National Level Cooperative Federations and examine various parameters of their functioning. The Committee was also to indicate the directions in which re-organization and re-orientation of federations is required in the context of emerging needs and the role of cooperatives in overall development, particularly in rural areas.

Recommendations

A cooperative federation is answerable to its constituent units and can justify its existence only in terms of the services it renders to those units.

NCUI Member Education Programme should be strengthened and financial responsibility shared by GOI, State Governments, Financial Institutions and cooperatives.

- NCCT Training should be strengthened and NCCT be de-linked from NCUI and reorganized on the lines of Swaminathan Committee. The possibility of corpus of funds should also be examined.
- NAFED should play a more important role as a leader of the cooperative marketing structure rather than as agent of government price support operations; undertake projects in backward areas for strengthening PAMS; play a more active role in spokesmanship and staff training.
- NCCF should conduct surveys of consumer needs to identify commodities that may be taken up by consumer cooperatives. The T&P Cell of the Federation needs further strengthening.
- Federations in the credit sector should develop their Research and Consultancy Wings and undertake micro level studies on simplification of loaning procedures, streamlining accounting methods, funds flow to weaker sections etc.
- The task of strengthening cooperative infrastructure devolves on institutions such as NDDB, NCDC and NABARD. However, where feasible federal responsibilities need to be transferred to concerned cooperative federations.
- District federations of labour cooperatives should be organized in all districts with 15-20 primary societies.
- National Federation of Industrial Cooperatives be divested of its cooperative character together with its formal status as a federation.
- Responsibility of benefiting weaker sections devolves on the entire federal structure.
- Inter-sectoral coordination through a "single window system" and linking of marketing of agricultural produce with distribution of consumer goods may be attempted.

- Members of National Federations should be limited to state level federation. Lower level cooperatives may be admitted as members on a wholly transitory basis where there are no state federations.
- Only experts to be nominated on the Board of cooperatives and nominated members should not have the right to vote in election.
- Provision in Section 29(3) permitting Chief Executives to represent their societies in General Bodies of the National Federations should be deleted.
- Administrators of cooperatives should not be eligible to vote.
- Sizes of Boards should be manageable and not exceed fifteen.
- Provisions of proviso (Section 22(d)) of MSCS Act may be availed by National Federations desirous of giving voting rights on equitable rather than equal basis.
- The Chairman of the General Body should be a person not from among the members of the Board. The General Body should be much larger than the Board of Management. General Body should have the power to review, check and issue binding directives on matters of policy.
- New cooperative national federations should be organized only for facilitating operations of its constituents, spokesmanship, promotional and consultancy work. Business functions should be taken up only to the extent entrusted by its units.

Agricultural Credit Review Committee (1989)

The Committee under the chairmanship of Prof. A.M. Khusro was to examine the problems of agricultural and rural credit, take stock of structural and operational deficiencies, constraints, quantitative and qualitative gaps and recommend major systemic improvements.

Recommendations

The Committee recommended:

- Prompt elections.
- Changes in Cooperative Law against protracted supercession.
- Completion of reorganization of primary societies based on viability norms, wherever the exercise has not been done.
- A programme of development for all such PACS which have not reached the loaning business of Rs 10 lakhs to be taken up for increasing its loan business, enlarging its package of profitable non-credit activities, augmentation of resources (deposits) and reduction in overdues.
- Improvement in quality of staff and accountability.
- Staff to be selected by societies.
- Incentive system.
- National Cooperative Bank of India.

The Committee has suggested that the Eighth Plan should, in fact, become the plan for revival of the weak primary agricultural credit societies.

Committee on Model Cooperatives Act (1991)

Appointed by the Planning Commission, Government of India under the chairmanship of Choudhary Brahm Prakash, the Committee which was expected to make a broad rapid review of the status of cooperative movement submitted its report in 1991 suggesting future directions and drafted a Model Cooperatives Act.

Recommendations

- State policy on cooperatives and the principles of cooperation have been stated in the beginning of the Act as a guide to the remaining provisions of the Model Cooperatives Act and to facilitate the government to conform to the basic ideology of cooperation.

- Procedure for Registration of a new cooperative is simplified and all artificial restrictions by way of area of operation, economic viability etc. are removed.
- The Model Cooperatives Act gives no rule making power to the government. The law itself lays down the broad parameters necessarily to be observed by cooperatives and leaves all other matters relating to constitution, management and business of the society to be conducted in accordance with its byelaws.
- The Model Cooperatives Act gives no power to the Registrar or the Government issue to orders for any of the following in a cooperative:
- Supersession of the Board of Director.
- Compulsory amalgamation or division of societies.
- Compulsory amendment of the byelaws.
- Veto/rescind/annul the resolution.
- Issue directives.
- Cooperative Federations/Unions are to assume greater responsibility towards the member cooperatives and in particular to ensure regular conduct of elections to the Board of Management and timely conduct of annual audit of accounts.
- The Role of the Registrar under the Model Cooperatives Act has been confined to the registration and liquidation of cooperatives, conduct of inquiry and in case of default to conduct elections, audit and to convene meeting of general body.

- The Model Cooperatives Act prohibits cooperatives from accepting funds from the Government by way of equity.
- To ensure the character of cooperative as a member user organization, special obligations have been imposed on members.
- Board of Directors have been made accountable for timely conduct of elections, regular convening of meetings of the managing committee and the general body and for participation therein and for the timely conduct of the audit of the books of accounts.
- Model Cooperatives Act prohibits officers of the Government to work in a cooperative.
- The Model Cooperatives Act provides for the Constitution of Cooperative Tribunal for settlement of disputes including appeals on matters relating to constitution, management and business of a cooperative and to take cognizance of any offence under the Act.

High Level Committee on Formation of Cooperatives Business as Companies (1999)

The Committee under the chairmanship of Y.K. Alagh was to draft a legislative framework to enable formation of cooperative business as companies and to convert existing cooperative business into companies under a regulatory framework similar to that a private limited companies. The Committee submitted its Report to the Government (Department of Company Affairs) on March 15, 2000.

Recommendations

- A statutory and regulatory framework that creates the potential for producer-owned enterprises to compete with other enterprises on a competitive footing. The Companies Act would provide for various forms of companies including private limited, public limited, trusteeship companies and nidhis, each with specific and appropriate provisions applicable to them, to provide for the formation and registration of producer companies which include the mutual assistance and cooperative principles within the more liberal regulatory framework afforded by the Company Law with suitable adaptations, and to provide an opportunity to cooperative institutions to voluntarily transform themselves into the new form of producer companies. This facility will be available to inter-State cooperatives whose objects extend to more than one State.

- Conversion of inter-State cooperatives to producer companies would be purely voluntary.
- Member equity may not be publicly traded, but may only be transferred, with the approval of the Producer Company's Board of Directors. Producer companies would not be vulnerable to take over by multinationals or other companies.
- The conversion option by inter-State cooperative society to producer company can be exercised only if two-thirds of the Members of the concerned society vote in favour of a resolution to that effect.
- The new form of company would be designated as "producer company" to indicate that only certain categories of persons can participate in the ownership of such companies. The members of the producer company have necessarily to be "primary producers", that is persons engaged in an activity connected with, or relatable to, primary produce.
- The objects of a producer company have been defined to include, among other things, production, processing, manufacture and sale of primary produces as well as allied matter.

- Provision for converted producer company to go back to the original fold of cooperative.
- In State Cooperative Laws, the Registrar's approval is required in most matters of governance and, especially, business. This regulatory and restrictive system presents significant obstacles to cooperatives being competitive in a market economy. Competing in a market economy requires speedy decisions on financial and administrative matters, for which autonomy is imperative, as is the case with other types of business, which conversion to producer companies will enable.

Committee on Urban Cooperative Banks (1992)

The Committee was set up in 1992 under the chairmanship of Marathe.

Recommendations

- Primary credit societies, which attained the revised entry point norms before 30 June 1993, be considered for inclusion in the list of functioning primary cooperative banks as a one time measure.
- Such societies should, thereafter, be taken up for inspection and considered for issue of licence based on merit.
- After the expiry of the cut off date of 30 June 1993, the primary credit societies, which do not satisfy the revised entry point norms should discontinue banking business and the concerned State Government should initiate necessary steps in this regard.

Task Force to Formulate Action Plan for Implementation of National Cooperative Policy (2002)

Based on the recommendations made at a Conference of State Ministers for Cooperation in 2001, the Government of India constituted a Ministerial Task Force to formulate a plan of action for implementation of National Cooperative Policy. The Task Force suggested that a single law instead of parallel laws should be introduced in the States. It also recommended among others that to depoliticize cooperatives, Members of Parliament or Members of Legislative Assemblies should not be allowed to hold office of any cooperative society.

Task Force for Reviving Rural Cooperative Credit Institution (2004)

In August 2004, the Government of India set up a Task Force to suggest an action plan for reviving rural cooperative credit institutions and legal measures necessary for facilitating this process. The Task Force, chaired by Prof. A. Vaidyanathan, has recommended that any financial restructuring without addressing the root causes of the weaknesses of the system would not result in its sustained revival. This would require legal measures for enabling cooperatives to evolve into democratic, self governing and financially well-managed institutions.

The recommendations of the Task Force in accordance with its Terms of Reference are basically confined to credit cooperatives. The revival package suggested by the Vaidyanathan Committee is a financial package for wiping off accumulated losses, covering invoked but unpaid guarantees given by State Governments, increasing the capital to a specified minimum level, retiring government share capital and technical assistance. It has also laid down the eligibility criteria for institutions, amongst which implementation of the recommendations for legal and institutional reforms is an important condition.

ANNEXURE-D

SALIENT FEATURES REGARDING COOPERATIVES DURING FIVE YEAR PLANS*

First Five Year Plan (1950-1956)

1. Cooperative method of organization should be adopted to the maximum possible extent for all the aspects of community development. The establishment of various types of cooperative societies will be the best means of enlisting the active support of the people on a voluntary basis for works of improvement on an organized scale.
2. Urban Cooperative banks to be developed to meet the credit and other needs of small entrepreneurs and cottage workers.
3. Establishment industrial cooperatives for workers since Agriculture alone cannot meet the employment needs in the rural areas. Aids in respect of power, implements, raw materials, technical advice and marketing facilities to all be made available to these societies.
4. To build up consumer's cooperatives over as wide a field of distribution as people.
5. The formation of housing cooperatives due to the strong urge towards urbanization.
6. Identified the need for diffusing knowledge of the principles and practice of cooperation among all ranks of cooperators. It recognized the need for specialized knowledge and technical skill for carrying out many of the managerial and supervisory function.
7. The plan stated that unless every department and every ministry accepts and adopts the policy of fostering cooperative

*NCUI, *Hundred Years of Cooperative Development in India*, pp. 77-84.

methods of business, rapid and enduring results cannot be obtained.

Hence, the first five year plan recommended that every department should follow the policy of building up cooperatives which may eventually replace the contractors or other middle men.

Second Five Year Plan (1956-1961)

1. The building up of a cooperative sector as part of the scheme of planned development is one of the central aims of national policy.
2. To enable the cooperative increasingly to become the principal basis for the organization of economic activity.
3. Such essential steps should be taken as would provide sound foundations for the development of agrarian cooperatives, so that within a period of 10 years or so, a substantial proportion of agricultural lands are cultivated on cooperative lines.
4. Programmes of cooperative development for the second five year plan were drawn up as broadly recommended by the Rural Credit Survey Committee.
5. The Plan shared the belief that Credit is only the beginning of cooperation. From credit, cooperation has to extend to a number of other activities in the village.
6. Every family in a village should be member of at least one cooperative society.
7. Cooperative movement should aim at making every family in the village credit worthy.
8. Linking of credit and non-credit societies to provide better services to the farmers.

9. Close lining up of procedure cooperatives and consumers cooperative for increasing rural incomes and employment and for raising rural levels of living.
10. Formation of labour and construction cooperatives in rural areas to replace the contract system and to generate more income and employment for the rural poor.
11. Recommended that people should be educated in the principles of cooperation and leading members of each community should be given special opportunities of training, so that they could assume fuller responsibility in the cooperative movement.
12. State governments and Universities should consider steps to introduce cooperative as a subject of instruction in educational courses at various levels.
13. The state should enter into partnership with cooperative institutions at various levels.
14. The second plan makes it clear that eh essential basis of state partnership in assistance and not interference or control.
15. Recommended establishment of a National Agricultural Credit (Long Term Operations) Fund with a view to facilitating the partnership of the State in cooperatives. Loans from this fund were to be advanced to states to enable them to subscribe to the share capital of cooperative credit institutions. The National Cooperative Development Fund established by the central government to enable the states to borrow for the purpose to subscribing to the share capital of non credit cooperative institutions.

Third Five Year Plan (1961-1969)

1. Cooperation should become progressively the principal basis of organization in many branches of economic life, notably in agriculture and minor irrigation, small industry and

processing, marketing, supply, housing, rural electrification and the provision at amenities for local communities.

2. To develop the village as the primary unit of organization in agriculture and many other economic and social activities which bear closely on the welfare of the rural population.
3. The specific programmes for cooperative credit and supplies, for marketing and processing, for consumer cooperative and for industrial and other cooperatives.
4. Proposed strengthening of the existing industrial cooperatives and to encourage the organization of new ones on sound lines. This included loans for working capital at a concessional rate of interest from government and central cooperative agencies and grants for managerial staff, improved tools and equipment.
5. Cooperatives should be organized on the basis of the village community as a primary unit. Where villages were too small, the number of villages to be served by a cooperative society could be increased in the interest of viability.
6. The plan stressed the importance of entrusting construction works, to the extent possible, to cooperatives and other voluntary organizations.
7. State and district cooperative unions should be strengthened to enable them to undertake more efficiently, cooperative training and education.
8. Recognised that Cooperation is a peoples' movement and the responsibility for the development of cooperation should devolve on higher organizations. The setting up of efficient federal organizations in all sectors of cooperative activity was suggested. As these organizations grow in strength, more power should be given to them and the cooperative department should limit their activities to audit, arbitration and inspection.

9. The regulatory power in relation to cooperatives may remain with the government, but some of them can be delegated to federal cooperative organizations.
10. The state should participate in the share capital of a primary society only if 60 percent of the members desired this, and it was supported by the central bank to which the society was affiliated. Wherever state participation in the share capital is direct, nomination of directors to the managing committee of primary societies should be avoided. If the nomination is considered essential, the authority should be delegated to central cooperative banks.

Fourth Five Year Plan (1969-1974)

1. Agricultural Cooperative on one hand and consumers cooperatives on the other hand occupied a central position in the 4th plan.
2. The plan stated that while it will be the responsibility of the cooperatives themselves to make the effort involved and reach those standards of efficiency to enable them to compete with other forms of organizations, the government should assist the cooperatives in important aspects such as finance, organization and trained personnel.
3. The plan accorded highest priority for reorganization of the primary credit cooperatives. It also recommended the rehabilitation and reorganization of the weak district central cooperative banks.
4. The plan stressed the need for effective supervision over the primary credit societies by the central financing agencies.
5. In order to favour the small cultivators, the plan proposed that society should give priority to the needs of the small cultivators. The long term loans to small farmers should be so phased that the repaying period is within their capacity.

6. Stress was given to the need for consolidation and strengthening of the existing marketing and consumer cooperatives.
7. The programme of cooperative training and education to be intensified. The existing cooperative training centres to be adequately equipped for training the requisite personnel. Efforts will be made to ensure that member education programmes for village cooperatives will be suitably supported and supervised by district central cooperative banks, marketing cooperative and other federations.
8. Recommended that it is necessary to have management pools in different sectors in each state to be operated by the federal organization. This was because at that time, a majority of the cooperative institutions were managed by personal on deputation from government.

Fifth Five Year Plan (1974-1979)

1. Make efforts towards the correction of regional imbalances in the level of cooperative development especially in the sphere of agricultural credit.
2. Make efforts towards restructuring and reorienting the cooperatives so as to shift the focus increasingly in favour of small and marginal farmers and other under-privileged sections of the people.
3. Strengthen the network of agricultural trained personal cooperatives (credit, marketing, supply and processing).
4. Recommended the formation of Farmers Service Cooperative Societies to help the small and marginal farmers.
5. Linking of credit with marketing.
6. Coercive action against willful defaulters.
7. Concessional finance through primary credit cooperatives to non-agriculturists and agricultural labourers.

8. Build up a viable consumer movement.
9. Need to develop a proper relationship between non-officials and the professional management.
10. Increased government support for strengthening the share capital base of the cooperative credit institutions.

Sixth Five Year Plan (1979-1985)

2. Re-examination of the existing cooperative policies and procedures with a view to ensuring that the efforts of the cooperatives are more systematically directed towards ameliorating the economic conditions of the rural poor.
3. To give greater coverage to the poorest among the target groups of the weaker sections; i.e., tenants, agricultural labourers and rural artisans.
4. A clearly drawn action programme for the strengthening of primary village societies so that they are able to effectively act as multi-purpose units catering to diverse needs of their members.
5. To continue with the reorganization of primary societies.
6. Strengthening the linkage between consumer and marketing cooperatives. Reorientation and consolidation of the role of the cooperative federal organizations so that they will be able to effectively support a rapidly diversifying and expanding agricultural sector.
7. Reorientation and consolidation of the role of the cooperative federal organizations so that they will be able to effectively support a rapidly diversifying and expanding agricultural sector.
8. Special attention for the development and strengthening of dairy, fishery and minor irrigation cooperatives.

9. Manpower development in small and medium cooperatives for the successful implementation of various programmes.

10. Development of professional manpower and appropriate professional cadres to man managerial positions.

11. The plan states the Panchayati Raj and cooperative institutions though various statutes. Of equal importance is the promotion of purely non-governmental organizations, which could motivate and mobilize people in specific or general development tasks. The role of government agencies should be help people to help themselves.

Seventh Five Year Plan (1985-1990)

1. Taking up of special Cooperative programs for implementation in the underdeveloped states specially in the North-Eastern Region.

2. Comprehensive development of primary agricultural credit societies to function as multi-purpose viable units.

3. Realignment of the policies and procedures of cooperatives to expand the flow of credit and ensure supply of inputs and services, particularly to the weaker sections, by making radical changes in the procedures and operational formalities followed for sanction and disbursement of credit.

4. Strengthening the primary agricultural credit cooperatives by appointment of a minimum complement of staff and provision of physical facilities.

5. Integrate the short term and long term credit structure.

6. Improve the recovery climate and reduction of overdues by giving more stress on the supervision over proper utilization of loans.

7. Strengthening the consumer cooperative movement in the urban as well as rural areas so that it can play a pivotal role in the public distribution system.
8. Focus on the maximum utilization of capacity of the cooperative processing units.
9. Consider the cooperative distribution of fertilizers as a service activity and not as a trading activity.
10. Promoting professional management and strengthening of effective training facilities for improving the operational efficiency.

ANNEXURE-E

NATIONAL BANK FOR AGRICULTURAL AND RURAL DEVELOPMENT (NABARD)

The National Bank for Agriculture and Rural Development (NABARD) Act was passed in 1981 and NABARD was set up to provide re-finance support to Cooperative Banks and to supplement the resources of Commercial Banks and Regional Rural Banks to enhance credit flow to the agriculture and rural sector.

The banks serves as an apex financing agency for the institutions providing investment and production credit for promoting the various development activities in rural areas.

Takes measures towards institution building for improving absorptive capacity of the credit delivery system, including monitoring, formulation of rehabilitation schemes, restructuring of credit institutions, training of personnel, etc.

Coordinates the rural financing activities of all institutions engaged in developmental work at the field level and maintains liaison with Government of India, State Governments, Reserve Bank of India (RBI) and other national level institutions concerned with policy formulation.

Undertakes monitoring and evaluation of projects refinanced by it.

NABARD's refinance is available to State Cooperative Agriculture and Rural Development Banks (SCARDBs), State Cooperative Banks (SCBs), Regional Rural Banks (RRBs), Commercial Banks (CBs) and other financial institutions approved by RBI. While the ultimate beneficiaries of investment credit can be individuals, partnership concerns, companies, State-owned corporations or cooperative societies, production credit is generally given to individuals.

ANNEXURE-F

PHASES OF COOPERATIVE DEVELOPMENT IN INDIA*

According to the Committee headed by C. Rangarajan on financial inclusion, 2008 the history of cooperative movement in India can be divided on four phases. In the First Phase (1900-30), the Cooperative Societies Act was passed (1904) and "cooperation" became a provincial subject by 1919. The major development during the Second Phase (1930-50) was the pioneering role played by RBI in guiding and supporting the cooperatives. However, even during this phase, signs of sickness in the Indian rural cooperative movement were becoming evident. The 1945 Cooperative Planning Committee had discerned these signs in the movement were becoming evident. The 1945 Cooperative Planning Committee had discerned these signs in the movement, finding that a large number of cooperatives were "saddled with the problem of frozen assets because of heavy overdues in repayment." Even so, also in the Third Phase (1950-90), the way forward was seen to lie in cooperative credit societies. The All India Rural Credit Survey was set up which not only recommended state partnership in terms of equity but also partnership in terms of governance and management. NABARD was also created during this phase. The Fourth Phase from 1990s onwards saw an increasing realization of the disruptive effects of intrusive state patronage and politicization of the cooperatives, especially financial cooperatives, which resulted in poor governance and management and the consequent impairment of their financial health. A number of Committees were therefore set up to suggest reforms in the sector.

*Report of the Committee on Financial Inclusion, p. 69.

Index

■■■